G000066568

REAL WORLD AI

REAL WORLD AI

A PRACTICAL GUIDE FOR
RESPONSIBLE MACHINE LEARNING

Alyssa Simpson Rochwerger
Wilson Pang

LIONCREST
PUBLISHING

COPYRIGHT © 2021 APPEN LIMITED

All rights reserved.

REAL WORLD AI

A Practical Guide for Responsible Machine Learning

ISBN 978-1-5445-1884-8 *Hardcover*
      978-1-5445-1883-1 *Paperback*
      978-1-5445-1882-4 *Ebook*

To our children.

Some might see us as an unlikely pairing. Wilson, born and raised in Qingdao, China, and Alyssa, born and raised in California, may never have crossed paths had it not been for our mutual interest in machine learning technology. It is with humility that we stand on the shoulders of the many who have come before us and attempt to simplify the complex and fascinating world that is machine learning technology for those who will come after us.

We believe fiercely that thoughtful, responsible, and ethical uses of machine learning technology can make the world a more just, fair, and inclusive place. We hope this book can be but one small contribution to that ongoing effort.

CONTENTS

INTRODUCTION

Alyssa

In late 2015, as a product manager within the newly formed computer vision team at IBM®, we were days away from launching the team's first customer-facing output. For months, we'd been working to create a commercially available visual-recognition application programming interface (API) that more than doubled the accuracy of existing models. The company had high hopes for scaling the API into a significant revenue stream. Our biggest focus to date had been improving the model's F1 score—a standard academic measure of a classification system's accuracy—against a subset of our training data, which included tens of millions of images and labels the team had compiled over months and years.

The API was meant to be used to tag images fed into it with descriptive labels. For example, you could feed it an image of a brown cat, and it would return a set of tags that would include "cat," "brown," and "animal." Businesses would be able to use it for all kinds of applications—everything from building user preference profiles by scraping images posted to social media, to ad targeting, or customer experience improvements. Over the past several months, to train and test the system, we'd used over 100 million images and labels from a variety of sources as training data. We'd succeeded in improving the F1 score considerably, to the point where an image I fed it of my sister and me at a wedding immediately came back tagged *bridesmaids*, which I thought was impressive.

And now, with all of IBM's release checklists completed and a planned launch mere days away, I was faced with an unanticipated problem.

That morning, I received a message from one of our researchers that was heart-stopping in its simple urgency: *We can't launch this.* When I asked why, he sent me a picture of a person in a wheelchair that he'd fed into the system as a test. The tag that came back?

Loser.

Panic. IBM has a 100-year history of inclusion and diversity. So, besides being objectively horrible, this output clearly indicated that the system did not reflect IBM's values. While we had been laser-focused on improving the system's accuracy, what other types of harmful and unintended bias had we accidentally introduced?

I immediately sounded the alarm, alerted my bosses, and scrubbed the launch. Our team got to work. Besides fixing the model, we had two main questions to answer:

How had this happened? And how could we make sure it would never happen again?

RESPONSIBILITY, NOT JUST ACCURACY

I was hired to the Watson division of IBM in October 2015 as the first product manager of the then-burgeoning computer vision team. As you may recall, Watson is the supercomputer that defeated *Jeopardy!*®[1] Champions Ken Jennings and Brad Rutter in 2011. Besides winning the $1 million jackpot, it gave the world one of the most public demonstrations of a machine learning system solving problems posed in natural, human language. When I joined the Watson team four years later, IBM was trying to expand that system into processing audio and visual information, hoping to generate a steadier stream of revenue than game-show winnings.

I was tasked with creating a strategic roadmap for com-

---

[1]   Jeopardy!® is a registered trademark of Jeopardy Productions, Inc.

puter vision in order to turn this largely academic pursuit into a real business. At the time, what IBM had created amounted to several different beta computer vision products in the Watson division, none of which were making much money or being used at scale. There were other uses of computer vision technology at IBM, such as the long history of Optical Character Recognition (OCR); the company's Advanced Optical Character Reader had been used by the USPS in New York City since 1975. But now, IBM customers were asking for more varied use cases that addressed an array of modern business needs.

At the same time, this team of a handful of engineers and researchers—some of whom had twenty years of expertise in the computer vision field—was debating how to improve the accuracy of machine learning models by trying different algorithms or model approaches. I was still trying to come up to speed on AI basics. I was a complete novice.

The questions I asked belied how new I was in the field. "After you try a new approach," I'd ask, "how will you know your result is more accurate than the last?"

No one could give me a straight answer. I wasn't sure if my lack of substantive experience in machine learning was to blame; after all, I was in rooms with highly experienced and talented people, and in comparison, I basically knew nothing on the topic. However, because I was the one who would have to explain to customers why the new system was better and more accurate, I persisted doggedly in trying to get an answer I could understand. After weeks of discussion and a crash course in how basic machine learning works and what training data is, we settled on an answer we could all get behind: you would know the system was more accurate when its F1 score improved.

So, that's where we placed all our focus. Our goal was to create an *accurate* system. And we did. We neglected to consider, however, whether we were introducing accidental bias into our training data. When the wheelchair image then came back with that disastrous tag, it was clear that we'd dropped the ball somewhere.

As a machine learning novice, I didn't fully understand what we had to do to prevent results like these. What was worse, it quickly became clear that no one on the team, myself included, was fully aware of what exactly was *in* the 100 million images of training data—the information we were training the model with. It was a huge oversight, and in retrospect, a big mistake.

To fix it, the team pulled together and divided up the tens of thousands of potential tags that could be returned for a given image and started going through them one by one. We'd pull up a group of images from a huge library, examine the tags that were returned, and use our human judgment to decide if the results were appropriate in a business context. After a lot of unplanned time and energy, we had found almost a dozen additional tags that we felt didn't align with our team's perspective, and certainly not with how we wanted IBM to be represented publicly. Fixing the problem involved removing those data points and completely retraining the system. It was arduous and time-consuming, but after several weeks, we managed to rid the output of the objectionable tags. We were able to go ahead with the product launch, confident that our system didn't contain offensive tag associations.

In retrospect, I got lucky with the resources I had at my disposal to solve that problem. I was working with a high-integrity, diverse, and talented team at a company with plenty of support. While our team was busy scrubbing unsavory tags by hand, our competition, including Microsoft® and Google®, endured some very public incidents of accidentally-racist output from their machine learning models. IBM avoided that particular catastrophe for the moment and managed to launch a system free from those problems, but not without spending a great deal of time and effort fixing the issue at the last minute. And without a robust system in place for proactively preventing the same problem in the future, it was bound to happen again.

SOLVING THE RIGHT PROBLEM

The good news was that we had narrowly avoided disaster. The bad news, however, was that the product wasn't a success.

Upon launch, the API didn't generate a significant revenue stream. The feedback we received from customers was that it simply wasn't accurate enough—our customers weren't able to use it to meaningfully power their businesses. This led to the second major "aha" moment in my AI career. When I dug into the customer problem and spent some time with our customers, I realized that even though we'd poured our time and effort into ensuring that the system was generally accurate, it still wasn't accurate enough for the narrower problems our customers were trying to solve. In most cases, they wanted something *extremely* specific. In one case, a chicken manufacturer wanted to distinguish between a chicken breast or thigh on the line using a fixed camera. When they fed it an image of the chicken packages, the tag of "chicken" or "food" that came back just wasn't going to cut it. In another case, an ice cream manufacturer wanted to know whether their new product label was present in a group of social media images—"ice cream," while correct, was far too broad.

In the end, we retooled the product into a system that could be trained individually for each customer with business-specific data. It would allow the chicken manufacturer to tell the difference between chicken breasts and thighs and the ice cream company to classify images according to specific criteria. This new API effort took six months of IBM's time and resources, but after the second major launch, it was dramatically more successful, scaling to significant revenue quickly. Customers could input small amounts of well-curated data and train a model to meet their needs within minutes. Now *that* was powerful, valuable, and innovative!

The problems my team at IBM faced in trying to launch profitable, scalable visual recognition AI aren't unique to that company or product. In fact, they're all too typical across businesses trying to create and scale AI solutions. Only 20 percent of AI in pilot stages at major companies make it to production, and many fail to serve their customers as well as they could. In some cases, it's because they're trying to solve the wrong problem. In others, it's because they fail to account for all the variables— or latent biases—that are crucial to a model's success or failure.

Wilson

I've been lucky enough to experience firsthand what it looks like when a company does it right with responsibly-built AI, and the results drive a massive increase in business. Meanwhile, I've also experienced big setbacks and challenges like the one Alyssa described many times in my career.

I joined eBay® back in 2006, and in 2009, the company was in very bad shape. Its share price was at a historical low, well off its near-$24 historical high; it was cutting costs, growth was negative, market share was shrinking, and the technology team wasn't empowered to innovate. Put simply, the company was in serious trouble.

They turned this around, largely thanks to investing in technology. They also brought in new perspectives: a new CEO, CTO, and several tech executives. In doing so, eBay started to make the engineering team an idea powerhouse and built it into an equal partner alongside the rest of the business. The company began the journey to use technology, data, and AI to drive business. I was lucky to join and build the search science team, which was one of the first few teams to leverage machine learning to optimize buyer experience and help them find desired items more easily on eBay's site. We focused on increasing *purchases per session:* the average number of items a buyer purchases in one user session. With that goal in mind, our AI model emphasized the sales (how many times an item was sold) over impressions (how many times an item was viewed), and those less expensive items were ranked higher than other items.

Our team had a huge amount of data at our disposal

and could easily A/B test new models to learn how they worked. And we had the luxury of seeing the results of our tests almost immediately.

Our team was locked and loaded.

We tried different machine learning models—models to rewrite buyers' queries, models to generate features to be used in the ranking model, and models to rank the final search results. We then ran a series of A/B tests to assess the model results, with great success. Many of the models proved that buyer conversion had increased. Other teams were motivated by these successes and started to put in the effort to increase their purchases per session. Everything looked rosy.

That is, until the finance team observed that those A/B testing wins didn't translate into increased revenue.

The initial try with AI in search science failed, and our team was pulled into a war room to understand why and we needed a solution—fast. We were hurting revenue for the company at a time when it couldn't afford to lose a single cent.

We dug deep into the search results for different queries and found one interesting phenomenon: very often, we ranked accessory items on the top. For example, many iPhone cases would rank at the top of the results when buyers searched the term "iPhone." Although those accessories were popular on the site, they weren't what the user had been searching for, so it created what we call "accessory pollution" and led to a bad user experience.

Aha! We had figured out why revenue had taken a dip; a $10 iPhone case represents *much* less revenue than a $300 iPhone. Our model was recommending the less expensive accessories when it should have been recommending the higher-priced phone.

PICK THE RIGHT MEASUREMENT

Success, much of the time, is all about what you choose to measure.

When we started our journey, the technology team unified different goals into one single goal focused on increasing sales. It's a very customer-centric choice to say your only goal is to sell more—but that's what sellers and buyers want and what we were ultimately paid to do.

After many rounds of discussions, we started with measuring the success by purchases per session. Our AI model succeeded in the goal but created a bad user experience and failed to deliver business growth. We needed to find a new solution with a different AI model, and even more importantly, a new way to measure the AI model's success. Clearly, "purchase per session" created the wrong motivation in our AI models and our team.

The lesson was obvious: be careful to pick the right measurement because it will inform the direction of your AI.

THE POWER OF DATA AND MACHINE LEARNING

Later on, we incorporated price-related signals to the model, which fixed "accessory pollution" problems. More importantly, we changed the measurement from purchase per session into GMV (gross merchandise value) per session.

Once our team showed the whole company how powerful machine learning and data could be, more teams started to leverage AI as the powerhouse for business growth. This ultimately had a huge impact on revenue and helped engineer the spectacular turnaround of the company. By 2012, eBay's share price had increased by 65 percent, and the company had enabled about $175 billion in commerce—around 19 percent of global e-commerce and nearly 2 percent of the global retail market.

eBay's foray into machine learning was aided by the massive database the company was able to use to train and quickly scale its AI initiatives. That's not an option for every company, nor does every company have the resources and infrastructure to apply to creating AI solutions—yet today, missing the boat on AI can quite literally mean losing the competitive edge in your industry. Tackling AI feels overwhelming and overly technical. How can you beat the market without washing out? And how can you ensure your AI development is responsible and its impact positive?

Fortunately, successful machine learning and responsible, ethical machine learning originate from the same process. Responsible, successful AI solutions don't have to be difficult. We created this book to help any organization reduce its risks on the journey to launching world-class AI.

In the chapters that follow, you'll learn a roadmap for how to launch responsible AI at scale. Alyssa and I will walk you through how to decide what problem to solve, why data matters and how to use it, best practices for success, how to scale, and how to consider security and ethics at every layer of development, execution, and maintenance.

WHO ARE WE?

Alyssa

Perhaps I'm an unlikely AI leader. I come to the field with a liberal arts degree in American studies—a student of culture and photography. I'm dyslexic, can't spell to save my life, and am fairly useless at coding—I know only enough to cause some damage but not enough to actually build anything functional. Back in 2015, several months before I was hired in the Watson division of IBM, I was serendipitously seated next to a successful and talented tech CEO as I was returning from a business trip on a flight home from London to San Francisco. I'd had a long week meeting with IBM customers in several different European cities and was eager to get home. Somewhere over the Atlantic, I struck up a conversation with her about technology, career paths, management, and life. When I asked for her advice on my own career's next steps, she offered me a guiding principle, which has stuck with me ever since.

"Go solve the hard problems," she said. "Everything else will sort itself out."

I took her advice and started to have a series of discussions with everyone and anyone from whom I could steal advice. I was looking for hard problems that resonated with me and a specific opportunity that aligned my passions, skillsets, and career aspirations. Unfortunately, few of the job opportunities available at the time fell into the "hard problem" category. Many of my mentors or advisors, who so generously lent me career advice, were encouraging me to pay my dues, gain more experience, or in some way seek prestigious titles or financially sound roles on traditional career paths. I found myself creating reasons to turn down director titles, lucrative stock options, or opportunities at red-hot, sexy startups. I kept thinking that while I had tremendous respect and admiration for the teams and individuals, I wanted to do more than optimize bottom lines. I wanted to be on a team solving a very "hard problem" that mattered. How could I channel my efforts to leave the world a better place?

This eventually materialized in the form of the Watson team at IBM. Now *here* was a hard problem that could be applied to address issues I cared about. Machine learning was a relatively new business field with high potential; I could get in on the ground floor and help shape a whole new market.

That first position on the Watson team kicked off a journey I'm still on today. As a product management leader at IBM, Appen®, and now Blue Shield of California®, I've focused on solving hard problems with data and machine learning techniques. It's incredibly rewarding work, not to mention worthwhile, with the speed of advancement AI lends to technology in general. Along this journey, I've placed a particular focus on responsible AI development. In order to avoid harmful and unwanted bias in outcomes, it's critical that organizations are empathetic, that they iterate throughout the model-building and tuning processes, and that they take great care with their data in order. Responsible AI isn't just better for the world; it's better for business outcomes, too.

I started my career as a developer with IBM, building large systems for banks, telecom operators, and securities exchange companies. I was excited by the power of software. As a developer, you're building your own world when you write software, and you have a degree of control and agency in building that world that's hard to find in most other careers.

I joined eBay after five years at IBM and continued to focus on engineering challenges to build eBay's billing and payment system. I then got the opportunity to join and build eBay's search science team to use machine learning and data to turn around the struggling business. In the beginning, I hesitated to switch my career to what seemed like an entirely new field. My mentor, a great tech leader who founded Bing's image and video search team and was leading the big turnaround at eBay, convinced me to go for the new challenge.

This was an inflection point for my career. For the next two years, I spent all my off time and weekends building my machine learning knowledge and picking up statistics. It was an intense period, but I learned the power of machine learning and how it can help change a business. After going deep in search science and delivering huge success in the vertical domain, I got the opportunity to lead a horizontal data service and solution team to enable data-driven decisions for every team in the company. I also built a retail science team and data labs to detect trends and seasonality of inventory, help sellers decide prices for their products, and help buyers find interesting products.

After 11.5 years with eBay, I joined Trip.com® as their chief data officer. My team used data and machine learning to optimize the travel experience. We made significant revenue increases through search, recommendation, and CRM. We also realized huge cost savings using AI in operations and customer service, improved internal efficiency in a big way, and set up the data foundation for the whole company. We were transforming the travel industry with AI and data.

Meanwhile, more and more industries had started to embrace AI and adopt machine learning solutions. As I watched people face new challenges to make AI work in the real world, I realized that I could make an impact by helping to accelerate the AI journey of businesses. This led me to join Appen as its Chief Technology Officer. Appen is the industry leader in the AI data field, and our mission is to create large volumes of high-quality training data *faster*, which solves the biggest challenge for AI practitioners—the lack of high-quality training data. We work with companies from all types of industries to help them deploy AI confidently. At Appen, our average pilot-to-production deployment rate for the past two years has been 67 percent—far better than the 20 percent general average. Building in AI responsibility and good data management from the beginning creates machine learning systems that are both more adaptable and more successful over the long-term.

WHAT YOU'LL LEARN IN THIS BOOK

AI represents a massive shift in technology, as revolutionary as electricity or the internet. Machine learning technology promises to reshape everything throughout the business world. Ten years ago, it was rare to find a restaurant that had a social media strategy; now, it's hard to find one that doesn't. Within a few years, it will be just as hard to find a company without an AI strategy. Companies that aren't working toward developing an AI strategy today are likely to fare as well as companies that decided not to pursue a web strategy in 2002 or a mobile strategy in 2008. It's absolutely required if you want to compete in the market.

We understand how overwhelming this can feel because we've been there. That's why we wrote this book: to demystify how to think about AI and provide an action plan for how to get started. Drawing on extensive multi-industry research, interviews with dozens of machine learning practitioners in startups and big companies, and our own real-world experience, we will help you design an AI system that serves your business case while remaining flexible and adaptable to changing circumstances. We won't teach you how to be a data scientist or select an AI model; you should hire experts to help with that. What we will do is help you understand what the best path to a successful strategy looks like and how to participate meaningfully as a business owner or decision-maker, setting you on a path for success.

This book will also provide line-of-business owners (like product managers) and team members on the more technical side (like engineers and data scientists) a starting place for a common language. We aim to bridge the gap between teams, providing business specialists and the C-level enough context to converse efficiently with technical implementers.

The path to responsible AI isn't straightforward, but with the aid of the best practices you'll learn in these pages, your chances of success are much higher. Using machine learning in your business to drive down costs and increase revenue doesn't have to be an overwhelming prospect. On the contrary, it's highly achievable. It's also a great motivator for any organization—it's interesting, fun, and produces big-impact outcomes. All it requires is a cross-functional team and an innovative spirit. You'll see dozens of examples of how it's been done well at companies around the world.

The key is to start small and make consistent progress.

From there, success with AI is more within reach than you think.

CHAPTER 1

THE BASICS OF AI–AND WHERE IT BREAKS DOWN

"Artificial intelligence is the science and engineering of making computers behave in ways that, until recently, we thought required human intelligence."

—ANDREW MOORE, FORMER DEAN OF COMPUTER
SCIENCE AT CARNEGIE MELLON UNIVERSITY

In August 2019, both Apple® and Goldman Sachs® were searching for solutions to an unforeseen problem after the launch of a hotly anticipated new product: the Apple credit card.

The card, with its touted ultra-security and sleek aesthetic, immediately saw a flood of applications, and by November, Goldman Sachs reported in its regulatory filings that it had issued $10 billion in credit to Apple Card holders.[2] But while early adoption by consumers was robust, a problem soon emerged: the Apple Card approval process was offering smaller lines of credit to women than to men. Basecamp Co-Founder David Heinemeier Hansson launched a series of tweets that went viral, claiming the Apple Card approved him for a credit limit twenty times higher than the one offered to his wife, even though they filed joint tax returns and his wife had a higher credit score. Apple Co-Founder Steve Wozniak shockingly tweeted back, "The same thing happened to [my wife and me]. I got 10x the credit limit. We have no separate bank or credit card accounts or any separate assets."

At first, no one at Apple seemed able to explain how the approval algorithm worked in order to analyze the output it was producing. Goldman Sachs claimed there was no gender bias in the approval process, the algorithm had been checked by a third party before the card was launched, and gender wasn't even an input on the application, so how could a gender bias affect the outcome?

Hansson countered, "Goldman and Apple are delegating credit assessment to a black box. It's not gender-

2   Shevlin, Ron. "If Tim Cook Won't Tell The World How The Apple Card Is Doing, I Will." *Forbes*, Forbes Magazine, 9 March 2020, www.forbes.com/sites/ronshevlin/2020/03/09/if-tim-cook-wont-tell-the-world-how-the-apple-card-is-doing-i-will/.

discrimination intent, but it is a gender-discrimination outcome."

Wired wrote in a November 2019 breakdown of the situation:[3]

> "A gender-blind algorithm could end up biased against women as long as it's drawing on any input or inputs that happen to correlate with gender. There's ample research showing how such "proxies" can lead to unwanted biases in different algorithms...other variables, such as home address, can serve as a proxy for race. Similarly, where a person shops might conceivably overlap with information about their gender."

In attempting to avoid bias by omitting gender as an input in the application, the Apple Card model builders accidentally set themselves up for the exact bias they were trying to avoid. If the input includes gender, the output can be tested to see if female and male inputs are treated differently by the model. However, without the critical "gender" input, the "gender-blind" model becomes just that: blind. There's no way to figure out what's going on with an obviously biased outcome.

Beyond illustrating the need for robust testing and mon-

---

3   Knight, Will. "The Apple Card Didn't 'See' Gender-and That's the Problem." *Wired*, Conde Nast, https://www.wired.com/story/the-apple-card-didnt-see-genderand-thats-the-problem/.

itoring of any AI model, this example also illustrates a fundamental truth of responsible AI: *it's difficult.* Even the biggest companies on the planet, with all the resources they have at their disposal, can run into big challenges. So if you're feeling like your company is struggling to understand how to enter the AI waters without taking on too much risk, you're not alone. As you'll see in the chapters that follow, not just Apple, but companies as large as Google, Walmart®, Tesla®, Microsoft, and dozens of others have had to continually overcome challenges as they went.

As a business expert, not a data scientist, you'll be most helpful in building any AI model by clarifying the importance of the inputs and deciding on the acceptable levels of confidence to meet business objectives. It's incumbent upon the data scientist to ask the right questions. Accuracy can suffer if the model tries to account for some variable that isn't actually important to the business case, but choosing to ignore that variable may be a business decision you can make to move things along.

Responsible AI isn't just good for your business; it's good for society. But AI is a complex enough field that to be able to build and deploy responsible AI, you must first understand the basics. Let's start with a brief walk-through of the foundations of AI.

HOW AI WORKS

When people are asked what AI is, the most common answer is "robots." Many don't realize that AI is nothing like Skynet and that they're probably interacting with AI every day.

When you're traveling for work and you take a picture of a receipt to expense it, a machine learning based computer vision system pulls information out of that picture and processes it.

When you call a support line and navigate the automated system by speaking to it, machine learning based speech recognition technology interprets your words and turns them into action.

As you scroll through Instagram on your phone, machine learning based search relevance is personalizing the content you see. When you post, another machine learning system analyzes your content and decides how to present it to your friends.[4]

When you use your phone to deposit a picture of a check, the money magically turns up in your bank account. Or, it *seems* like magic. In reality, a complex array of machine

---

4   Hu, Yajing, "The Mystery Behind Instagram Recommendation System." Spring 2019, https://blogs.commons.georgetown.edu/cctp-607-spring2019/2019/01/28/ the-mystery-behind-instagram-recommendation-system/.

learning made it happen: first, a computer vision system analyzed the image and turned the text into numbers. Then, a fraud detecting system evaluated whether or not your session was likely to be fraudulent and made the call on whether to allow the bank to credit the money to your account. Once these checkpoints were successfully passed, the money was deposited.

And, of course, every time you talk to Siri®,[5] Alexa®,[6] or Google Assistant®,[7] machine learning speech recognition is interpreting what you say and—more or less—making it happen.

All of these are simple, often seamless, interactions. Most of the time, you're not even aware of the fact that you're using AI-based systems—it just happens without you needing to know any of the details behind the scenes. They're often designed to passively interact with you, understand the information you give them, and suggest or guide you toward the outcome you intended.

Artificial intelligence isn't just one thing. It refers to an evolving collection of technologies; the definition of AI continues to change as the technology changes.

---

5   Siri® is a registered trademark of Apple, Inc.

6   Alexa® and all related logos are registered trademarks of Amazon.com, Inc., or its affiliates.

7   Google Assistant® is a registered trademark of Google, LLC.

Modern AI began much further back in history than one would think; classical philosophers used symbols to describe human thinking and attempted to envision models of human intelligence. What we call AI, however, only became a formalized field of study at a Dartmouth College conference in 1956. There, the term "artificial intelligence" was coined.[8] The field has gone through multiple feasts and famines; after two "AI winters" between the early 1970s and the early 1990s, AI study took off again in the late 90s. Since then, we've seen a computer beat the world's greatest chess player and the reigning *Jeopardy!* Champion at their own games, and now, in 2021, millions of us ask small devices in our homes or on our wrists for the weather, directions, or cooking instructions in natural language. And the devices politely answer back—only sometimes incorrectly.

AI refers broadly to machines that perform functions that, when performed by humans, require intelligence.[9] Whereas *machine learning*, a subset of AI, specifically describes *algorithms* that can get better at something without explicitly being programmed to do it—algorithms can learn from the data they are fed (like the Apple Card approval algorithm). And *deep learning*, which is repre-

8   Knapp, Susan, Dartmouth College, December 2008, http://www.dartmouth.edu/~vox/0607/0724/ai50.html.

9   Valencia, Jean Pierre, "Understanding The Difference Between AI, Machine Learning, and Deep Learning." *Tangocode*, 17 July 2019, tangocode.com/2019/07/ai-machine-learning-and-deep-learning/.

sented by the most sophisticated AI systems, often takes the form of artificial neural networks modeled after the basic architecture of the human brain. Deep learning systems can accomplish complex tasks like looking at a single photo uploaded by a guest at a hotel and identifying multiple elements that classify the photo for the use of other guests—food, location, weather, and so on.

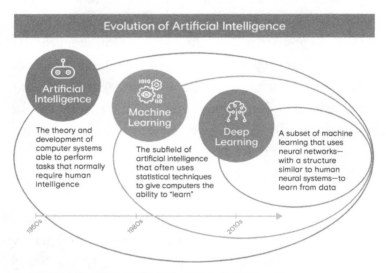

AI vs. Machine Learning vs. Deep Learning from Lynn Heidmann[10]

AI is often poorly understood as a black box. Something goes in one end, and magic comes out the other. This "black box" thinking is only partially accurate—the box isn't actually opaque. Typically, when people say "black

---

10   Heidmann, Lynn. "AI vs. Machine Learning vs. Deep Learning." *Blog*, blog.dataiku.com/ai-vs.-machine-learning-vs.-deep-learning.

box," they are referring to a model or algorithm that's been trained within a limited dataset; it's what Hansson was referring to when he called out the biased Apple Card algorithm. Inputs are fed in, and the model is taught what the expected answers are. With enough data, the model will learn the similarities and differences between the inputs. After training, the model can accept inputs it has never seen before and produce, with some degree of confidence, corresponding outputs. Its output is wholly dependent on the quality of the data input that was curated by humans, similar to how a toddler models the adult behavior that it sees—hopefully, *please* and *thank you*, but occasionally, perhaps, a swear word.

TRAINING VS. INFERENCE

How do you get machine learning models? You train them.

Imagine you have a new puppy. You want the dog to sit down every time you say, "Sit." You repeat the command and give your dog a treat whenever it connects the dots and gets it right. After a while, the dog will infer that it is time to sit whenever it hears the word "sit."

What happens with AI is very similar. You teach AI how to get it right. The teaching process is called model training, and the only difference is the teaching target: a model instead of a puppy.

Data scientists load a lot of data into a machine, and the machine tries to choose a model to "fit" the data. The model or algorithm can range from a simple equation (like the equation of a line) to a very complex system of logic/math that gets the computer to the best predictions. The training process decides all the parameters (weights and bias) in the equation.

Choosing the right model and finding its parameters can be a challenging job. Data scientists used to work on a lot of the details of the math formula, produce low-level matrix calculations, write a lot of code, and spend a huge amount of time debugging the code. Frameworks like TensorFlow® or PyTorch® have simplified the work dramatically. These frameworks offer ready-made building blocks that significantly improve the speed at which even newcomers can implement machine learning architectures and train a decent model quickly.

Now you have a well-trained model, and you want it to make a prediction when you feed it new data. The process of using a trained machine learning algorithm to make a prediction is called "inference."

However, there are many steps between model training and model inference. You need to package your model, deploy it to production, monitor its performance, and refresh it if you see a performance drift. Real-world AI needs an organization to build an environment and culture to enable all these operations efficiently. The new, emerging practices to streamline managing the machine learning life cycle are called MLOps.

SUPERVISED, UNSUPERVISED, AND REINFORCEMENT LEARNING

Although deep learning is the most popular machine learning model nowadays because of its far-reaching applications, it is also important to know that many other traditional machine learning models are still used in different scenarios.

Let's take a look at another popular machine learning model: the decision tree. A person is trying to make a decision: should I go to my colleague's party? A few pieces of information will go into that decision: Am I free? Is it going to be fun? Is it near public transit? In the end, the person will decide based on the answers to those inputs, each of which you could think of as a layer of the overall question.

The person will try to answer each of these questions. Some will be yes, some no. Some are more important than others—if it's going to be fun, maybe it matters a lot less if it's near public transit. There's an intrinsic weight to each of these inputs, and the person will answer the question by doing some mental math to combine them all; if the result passes some threshold, they'll go to the party.

Humans weigh these factors and arrive at a decision without even thinking about it, but computers have to be told explicitly how to make a decision. It's very important that the data scientists and business people responsible for the creation of a model clarify and articulate the thresholds of decision-making ahead of time because the model's decisions are only as good as the inputs it knows about.

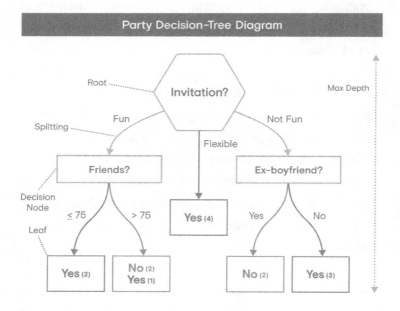

Perhaps this would-be partygoer learns their former significant other will be there. That might sway the decision to an absolute "no," regardless of the other answers. But a decision tree created to decide whether or not to go to parties wouldn't take that input into account unless it had a layer to handle former partners and had been trained on some examples.

The creation of this party-decision tree is based on *supervised learning*. The overwhelming majority of AI-use cases in the business world use supervised learning models. This is a fancy way of describing algorithms that are trying to mimic human decision-making in specific scenarios using data that previous humans have created as the training data. This is because there are many tasks in business that are repetitive, hard to scale, annoying, low-value, or simply take too long when performed by humans. If a computer can do the same thing in less time, much more scalably, then wouldn't we want to use it instead of a person?

Unsupervised learning, in contrast, is trained on data that have no right answers. It uses algorithms to find the inherent, latent structures in the data.

And a third common model is *reinforcement learning*. Reinforcement learning, rather than being trained on data, requires the model to be set up to learn by *doing* through trial and error. The model is rewarded when it makes decisions that lead to good outcomes, and over time, it discovers how to give correct answers more and more frequently.

YOUR ROLE IN BUILDING AI

Too often, an AI project idea makes its way from conception to implementation through a game of organizational telephone. The path from the original business stakeholder who dreams it up to the machine learning engineer or data scientist who will actually build it inevitably passes through five steps and three management changes. In the end, the person who's building the model often doesn't understand and can't articulate the business context of the project they're working on. When they need to make trade-offs or strategic decisions, there's no guarantee they'll make ones that will work in production. At worst, they'll end up diverging from the original goal.

A machine learning industry expert had an experience that exemplifies organizational telephone games and the kind of damage they can cause. In his early days of working with machine learning, he supported a project with an app that allows users to monitor their health. It encourages users to record all the food they eat in the app to help monitor consumption.

He was given the task of building a model to classify the foods users entered into the app into groups, such as fruits, vegetables, etc., so the app could better understand which foods users were entering. This was a classic natural language processing (NLP) task. Because users entered foods into the app manually, people would spell "apple" with three p's or "banana" with three n's, and so on.

His assignment was to create order out of this messy, real data. Eager to be successful and prove himself, he dove right in to creating that order. He spent more than six weeks cleaning the data and creating mappings from the messy reality into a clear hierarchy, only to find out the groupings he had created were not at all what the product team needed or wanted. So, he had to start over from square one. Time and resources had been lost because no one had told him which groups the app could actually monetize, and the groups he had created were worthless from a business standpoint. Despite his ambition and hard work, he nevertheless wound up asking an all-too-common question: "Why the hell didn't anybody tell me about this?"

The reason he didn't have the information he needed was the business folks—the product team—had not been in close contact with the person executing the AI model, and because of this, the project completely stalled for weeks on end. As a businessperson, your job is to get involved granularly, helping to specifically define the outcomes that are important to the business.

It might be surprising to learn that, in fact, the bulk of the work of creating a model is making those kinds of decisions about the acceptable thresholds for the model's output. If data of high enough quality is available, and the inputs and outputs have been well articulated, the actual data scientist's work of creating and training the model shouldn't take days or weeks. Lots of good tooling exists—such as Databricks, Weights & Biases, and IBM AI 360—to make the process of iterating and refining the model to the expected level of accuracy much easier than it was even just a few years ago. Your data science team should take advantage of these types of tools. It's a fast-changing landscape.

As you're making these choices about the scope of your model, it's important to consider the ethical implications of its decisions. If you've decided to optimize your model to the point where it's 90 percent accurate, that means that 10 percent of the time, it's getting the decision wrong. If your model is classifying support tickets as higher or lower priority, maybe that 10 percent isn't such a big deal. But if it's identifying reports of sexual assault, misclassifying 10 percent could represent a significant ethical failure, not to mention the introduction of substantial liability. Take the example of Uber®, which uses a system called COTA (Customer Obsession Ticket Assistant) to classify its support tickets.[11] COTA uses machine learning and NLP (Natural Language Processing) to quickly evaluate whether a ticket

---

11   Molino, Piero; Wang, Ya-Chia; Zheng, Huaixiu, "COTA: Improving Uber Customer Care with NLP & Machine Learning", January 2018, https://eng.uber.com/cota/.

is about a technical issue with the app, a fare dispute, or any of the other thousands of possible types of issues that commonly arise for customers and drivers on the platform. Once it knows what type of issue it's dealing with, COTA routes the ticket to the correct team in order to get it addressed. While human agents are backing up COTA, it's still crucial that the system avoids misclassification as much as possible—the risk of even one sexual assault complaint getting routed to the technical support team is far too great. In the development of a tool like COTA, business-focused roles like that of Product Manager are key. The data science team is focused on making the model faster and more accurate across the board—but the person focused on business objectives is going to be the crucial voice when it comes to defining how to balance speed, risk, and accuracy.

If you're introducing a model that used to do something that relied on humans making ethical decisions, you'll want to guard against your data science team being too homogeneous. The job of the data scientist is essentially to encode intentional bias into the model to make a decision; that's how decisions are made. If the humans supplying the data and creating the algorithms introducing that bias don't consider enough context on sensitive areas that usually rely on human judgment, they could introduce unintentional bias.

Also, recall Microsoft's Twitter chatbot, Tay, which used

reinforcement learning to get better at conversation, but whose training wasn't secured against bad actors. Tay was a research project by two teams at Microsoft to explore conversational understanding. The chatbot used AI and content written by a dedicated human staff to form its responses and develop conversational patterns. But Tay's biggest source of data was relevant, public data that had been anonymized and filtered. In essence, Tay was supposed to learn how to converse with humans through Twitter by studying the user-generated dialogues tweeted at her. As Microsoft stated when launching Tay, "The more you chat with Tay, the smarter she gets."[12] Unfortunately, there was no filter on exactly what Tay could or would learn from fellow Twitter users. As a result, Tay was fed a million malicious conversation examples by 4chan. It ended up becoming an extremist chatbot that promoted Nazism. In many cases, Tay was simply repeating inflammatory lines that had been tweeted at it. However, the more racist and profane content fed to Tay, the more racist and profane it became by virtue of her programming and lack of any filter applied to what was relevant conversation and what was trash or moderation of data inputs.

AI isn't magic. It's a collection of technologies that can be harnessed to make decisions that serve a set of goals.

---

12   "Tay, Microsoft's AI Chatbot, Gets a Crash Course in Racism from Twitter." *The Guardian*, Guardian News and Media, 24 Mar. 2016, www.theguardian.com/technology/2016/mar/24/tay-microsofts-ai-chatbot-gets-a-crash-course-in-racism-from-twitter.

We all use AI in our everyday lives, so the way models are designed matters. The results you get matter. A lot more than just data science goes into a model's creation—business decisions make up the most significant portions of the work involved. Choosing the model's parameters and scope and determining when its accuracy is good enough to support the business case, when and how to deploy it, and how to monitor its performance are crucial to its success.

Consider a healthcare scenario of matching patient records. When a person shows up at a hospital, it's helpful and sometimes critical in order to deliver life-saving care for doctors to have the patient's medical history at their fingertips so they can better understand their current medical condition. Consider the scenario where perhaps the patient has changed addresses since their last visit to the hospital, or perhaps they got married and changed their name, or perhaps they simply abbreviated their address on the intake form slightly different from the last time they were at the hospital.

	RECORD 1	RECORD 2	RECORD 3
NAME	John Doe	John Doe	Jon Doe
DATE OF BIRTH	1/1/1980	01/1/1980	01/01/1980
ADDRESS	1500 Main Street	1500 Mn St	1500 Maine St
CITY	NY	New York	New York
STATE	NY	NY	NY

Hospitals commonly use machine learning based models to do patient record matching. In this case, you can see that the three records are not an exact match, but as a human evaluating this, you can tell that it's highly probable that the three records are from the same person. A machine learning system might not have the same level of confidence. As a businessperson working with AI, it's appropriate for you to ask questions like, "What is the risk if we accidentally match up records where it wasn't the same person?" Or, "Is it riskier *not* to match up records when it was likely the same person, causing the doctor to miss a key piece of historical medical data?"

Business logic, data transformation, and confidence thresholds must be set up to make a series of decisions that lead to the logical machine learning based conclusion that all three records are of the same person. It's critical to be a part of these decisions and talk about the business and customer implications of how they are weighted and decided.

Like everything else in business, AI is only a tool. It's only as valuable as what it can do for your business.

A FAILURE OF OBJECTIVES

It's not uncommon—in fact, it's shockingly *common,* even among businesses seasoned in AI work—that a huge investment of money and resources is made in an AI solution, only to have it produce the wrong result or even fail completely. A company can do all the "right" things, hire smart and experienced people, and have the best intentions, and still wind up expensively spinning their wheels rather than achieving objectives.

Case in point: in October of 2013, IBM announced an exciting partnership with the University of Texas's MD Anderson Cancer Center. The alliance would use Watson's cognitive computing system to take cancer research to new heights. After more than three years of work and more than $62 million spent by MD Anderson, the project was put on hold, having never actually used the technology on a patient.[13]

One of the reasons was that the MD Anderson team incorrectly identified and failed to deeply understand the specific problem that AI had the potential to impact. Applying machine learning to an objective as broad as "cure cancer" will quickly reveal the limitations of the technology. An AI model needs a specific problem to solve in the present, not a faraway future goal. This is partly because AI isn't a "set it and forget it" type of system that will keep churning out results without human interven-

13   Herper, Matthew, "MD Anderson Benches IBM Watson In Setback For Artificial Intelligence In Medicine", *Forbes*, February 2017, https://www.forbes.com/sites/matthewherper/2017/02/19/md-anderson-benches-ibm-watson-in-setback-for-artificial-intelligence-in-medicine/?sh=ce83e7a37748.

tion. It requires constant maintenance, management, and course-correction to continue to provide meaningful, desired output. Without having a clear idea of the objectives, success measurements, carefully defined expectations, milestones, and guidelines when embarking on a project, the chances of success are slim—as MD Anderson discovered.

This is one of many examples of how the siren call of AI—promising incredible solutions but lacking intentionality in execution—can lead companies down a dangerous road of wasted time and money. When this happens, it's common to reflexively conclude that investing in AI at all was a mistake. And after reading stories of missing the target on desired results like those of Apple and MD Anderson, you're probably wondering how you can avoid the same pitfalls.

The answer is that failure is not inevitable. People make AI, and people train AI systems with data collected and prepared by people. Smart and effective AI is wholly within your control, as is designing and training effective systems that produce desired results.

If you intentionally and responsibly design your AI to solve a specific, valuable business case, it will be more successful, and it will serve your users better.

WHEN GOOD AI GOES BAD

Sometimes, even when objectives and goals are clearly defined, end users are let down by the technology, and the harmful effects are felt not just by the business but by society as a whole. Biases in race, gender, class, and other markers have made their way through to the output even in systems created with careful intention.

GOOGLE TRANSLATION

In 2018, Google launched a targeted initiative to reduce gender bias in its translation software, which runs on a deep learning model called *neural machine translation* (NMT). Why was there gender bias in the model in the first place? The model learns from hundreds of millions of pieces of data across hundreds of languages—already-translated bits of text. But different languages have different treatments for masculine and feminine word forms. This ultimately taught the model to deliver a masculine translation when fed words like "strong" or "doctor" and to deliver a feminine translation when fed words like "nurse" or "beautiful." So, although the input in Turkish, which uses gender-neutral pronouns, would be "o bir doktor," the output in English would automatically translate "*he* is a doctor." In the absence of being able to alter the input, Google's fix was on the output—any time a gender-neutral input is given, the English results will include both forms, i.e., "he is ____" and "she is ___."

Google Translate's gender bias is deeper than this; however, when fed long strings of sentence constructions following the template "[gender-neutral pronoun] is [adjective]," the results are worrying. For example, the adjective "hardworking" will assign a "he." The adjective "lazy" will assign a "she."[14]

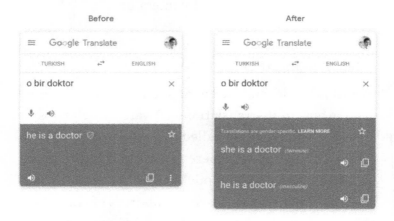

The company has articulated every correct intention in promoting fairness and avoiding bias in its translation tool, but because its training data is the vast corpus of human language, the model's lessons are heavily influenced by gender conventions around the world. Google's task, then, is a continuous focus on accounting for biased inputs by curating outputs.

---

14   Lee, Dami. "Google Translate Now Offers Gender-Specific Translations for Some Languages." *The Verge*, The Verge, 6 Dec. 2018, www.theverge.com/2018/12/6/18129203/ google-translate-gender-specific-translations-languages

Amazon began a large-scale project in 2014 that aimed to automate the review of job applicants, using AI to score candidates on a scale of 1 to 5. Especially with the incredibly high volume of applicants and resources required to evaluate them, the need and push for such an automation tool was high. As an Amazon insider put it to Reuters, "Everyone wanted this holy grail...an engine where I'm going to give you 100 résumés, it will spit out the top five, and we'll hire those."[15]

After a year of work, Amazon realized there was a problem with its system. The model was trained to evaluate candidates by learning from patterns sourced from résumés submitted in the past ten years. But gender diversity was a relatively new emergence in the field; most of those résumés had been submitted by men. As a result, the model learned that male candidates were preferable and penalized any applications that included the word "women's," such as mentions of women's sports teams or extracurricular activities on submitted résumés.

By 2017, Amazon had to abandon the tool. There was no data they could use to train the model that wouldn't result in a gender-biased outcome. Instead, the company

---

15 "Amazon Ditched AI Recruiting Tool That Favored Men for Technical Jobs." *The Guardian*, Guardian News and Media, 10 Oct. 2018, www.theguardian.com/technology/2018/oct/10/amazon-hiring-ai-gender-bias-recruiting-engine.

pivoted to a different solution: they developed an AI tool that spotted current candidates worth recruiting across the internet. To train the model, they fed it past candidate résumés and taught it to recognize certain career- and skill-related terms.

It *still* resulted in bias. Because the model was trained on mostly men's résumés, it learned to favor words more commonly used by men to describe their skills and responsibilities. The candidates returned by the web crawler were overwhelmingly men. Amazon shut down the project.

In both of Amazon's cases and Google Translate's case, the companies *were* being good corporate citizens; each company monitored the results, listened to user feedback, and responded quickly. That's responsible AI.

PAROLE DECISIONS

One of the most classic examples of unfair bias in a machine learning tool is the COMPAS software—Correctional Offender Management Profiling for Alternative Sanctions. The software was created to measure the likelihood of a criminal becoming a repeat offender, and the outcomes are used to help judges make parole decisions. It is literally the difference between continued imprisonment and freedom. In 2014, ProPublica examined the algorithm that powers COMPAS. What they found was deeply disturbing: the COMPAS score was completely unreliable in predicting future crimes. Only 20 percent of the people who scored likely to recommit a violent crime actually did. And when misdemeanors were factored in, the score's accuracy barely edged out a random flip of a coin.

More troubling—and far more harmfully impactful to a specific group of people—was that the COMPAS formula overwhelmingly labeled Black defendants as high-risk future criminals more often than white defendants, no matter the difference in their crimes. Brisha Borden, a teenager with a clean record from the suburbs of Fort Lauderdale, was arrested and charged with petty theft for picking up and riding an unlocked push scooter for a few minutes, which was determined to belong to a six-year-old neighbor. She was assigned a high-risk score of 8. Whereas forty-one-year-old Vernon Prater, who had already served five years in prison for armed robbery when he was arrested for shoplifting from Home Depot, was assigned a low-risk score of 3. Borden is Black; Prater is white. Consistent racial disparities in risk assessment results were found in staggering numbers.

The privately-owned company that created the software used in Borden and Prater's cases, Northpointe, defended its model. The score is created from a survey of 137 questions. Like the Apple credit application, which intended to avoid gender bias by not asking about gender, the assessment questions do not include an identification of race.

> The survey asks defendants such things as: "Was one of your parents ever sent to jail or prison?" "How many of your friends/acquaintances are taking drugs illegally?" and "How often did you get in fights while at school?" The questionnaire also asks people to agree or disagree with statements such as "A hungry person has a right to steal" and "If people make me angry and I lose my temper, I can be dangerous."[16]

The software behind COMPAS wasn't originally designed to be used in a court setting, an objective that would certainly have an impact on the training and testing of the model. Responsible building and use of such a system must include a consideration of fairness. These are commercial tools that are making decisions that profoundly affect people's lives. It's often an irresponsible decision to use a model for a purpose that it wasn't specifically designed for.

WITH GREAT POWER...

AI represents the largest technological shift many of us will see in our lifetimes. It's transforming the world on every level, from moment-to-moment interactions people

---

16   Julia Angwin, Jeff Larson. "Machine Bias." *ProPublica*, 23 May 2016, www.propublica.org/article/machine-bias-risk-assessments-in-criminal-sentencing.

have with devices in their homes to large-scale decisions made by global organizations that affect millions of people. With such widespread power inherent to the technology, it's the responsibility of those creating AI solutions to ensure that their AI is ethical, safe, and in service to the world—essentially, that it makes the world a better place, not a worse one.

Responsible AI isn't just good for business; it's good for the world. In the next chapter, you'll learn how to develop an AI strategy that will incorporate responsible AI development into every facet of your business.

CHAPTER 2

DEVELOPING AN AI STRATEGY

"Success in creating AI would be the biggest event in human history. Unfortunately, it might also be the last, unless we learn how to avoid the risks."

—STEPHEN HAWKING

While you're trying to solidify what you want to achieve and why, keep in mind that AI isn't a goal in and of itself. It's a very powerful tool and often transformational, but the strategy you develop should pursue a business goal. It's silly to sprinkle AI on a project for its own sake.

Wilson

During the 11 years I worked at eBay, the company moved toward more structured and scalable systems, processes, and teams across the entire organization. It didn't happen overnight but rather as a result of the application of a carefully considered, holistic strategy. After the great turnaround, eBay wanted to expand the adoption of data and machine learning into more domains. However, it was challenging to enable different organizations to accelerate their AI initiative without a holistic AI strategy.

Before the transformation, it took my team as long as several months to develop and launch a new model from conception to production. I had a wonderful team who worked very hard, but the company wasn't set up to allow us to procure infrastructure quickly or collect data from departments across the organization—a problem still common in many organizations. These inefficiencies created enormous delays, leading us to worry about remaining competitive in the market. Of course, other teams throughout the company had the same problems.

In 2015, eBay made the decision to implement a common, unified vision for a data-driven organization by investing in the creation of an internal platform for unified AI that would come to be known as Krylov. eBay put together a team to guide the initiative, comprising members of the AI platform team, which would build and provide the service; the infrastructure teams, who would provide the dependencies of the platform; and the AI domain teams, who would actually use the platform and could speak to use cases.

The domain teams were assembled from all across the company. Advertising, computer vision, risk, marketing, finance—anyone who had an interest in shaping the platform to serve their future AI needs.

The team worked together to develop a complete strategy and roadmap. During the discovery phase, they analyzed challenges throughout the company that inhibited effective AI. They worked with AI researchers to understand their day-to-day processes. They identified data silos throughout the organization and figured out how to break them down.

The strategy they developed, which they intended to fulfill over a period of several years, included requirements for an enormous, centralized training cluster with secure access to data. It detailed the need for a platform to automate the training and deployment of models throughout their life cycle. It described a universal data life cycle abstraction that encompassed data discovery, preparation, and storage.

The strategy also established tenets that would allow the many diverse use cases and processes throughout the company to use the platform, including support for any number of software frameworks or hardware needs, a focus on scale, and a commitment to open source technologies.

The implementation of this platform, of course, didn't

happen overnight. They started small, building discrete projects that, while useful on their own, helped build up the overall development of the platform as well. Teams throughout the company were assigned tasks with clear, measurable, and achievable metrics that were meaningful to the business organization they were a part of.

In order to popularize the AI vision, as well as increase familiarity with its specifics, we instituted a program that allowed any engineer in the company to embed themselves into the AI platform team to help build it. Not only did this educate our workforce on the concepts and technologies and scale up the skills of our employees, it also provided a channel for feedback on the platform itself.

At this point, Krylov had dramatically improved eBay's ability to develop AI. Instead of the year it used to take teams to bring a model from idea to production, it now took only days. Centralized governance reduced the company's liability and allowed it to manage the massive amounts of data that moved through its system. The rapid development of features has allowed eBay to retake its position as a leader in the market, and the culture and infrastructure they've created allow them to adapt their features as rapidly as customers' needs change.

eBay has, so far, been highly successful in their transition to an AI-led company because they developed a cohesive, holistic strategy. But they didn't roll it out as one huge effort; they pursued their ultimate goal by solving specific problems with measurable impact. Knowing what you want to achieve, why you want to achieve it, and why it's important will set your team up for success.

AI FOR ITS OWN SAKE

At the 2016 Met Gala, Marchesa, a fashion brand specializing in women's clothing, debuted what they called a "cognitive dress." Some weeks prior to the event, they had partnered with IBM's Watson division to develop a dress that incorporated AI in some way. The result was a high-fashion dress covered in LEDs, which lit up in different colors. The patterns of the lights were determined in real-time by Watson, which analyzed the tone and sentiment of tweets about the dress, and transmitted the results to a small computer embedded in the fabric. If the tweets were positive, the lights would behave in one way, and if they were negative, they'd do something else. This dress wasn't made to be sold; it was merely an excuse to sprinkle AI onto fashion.[17]

Did Marchesa achieve anything with their cognitive dress? If the goal was to somehow add AI to a piece of cloth-

---

17   Stinson, Liz, "IBM's Watson Helped Design Karolina Kurkova's Light-Up
      Dress for the Met Gala", *Wired*, May 2016, https://www.wired.com/2016/05/
      ibms-watson-helped-design-karolina-kurkovas-light-dress-met-gala/.

ing, then one could argue the answer is "yes." It certainly generated a lot of publicity for both Marchesa and IBM, although no further AI partnerships developed. But the AI piece of the dress wasn't particularly complicated, nor did it serve any business purpose.

In contrast, an elite fabric company based outside of Milan married AI with fashion in a way that greatly enhanced its business. A major part of their business involves designing and supplying raw fabric materials for high-end fashion designers such as Gucci and Louis Vuitton. Their campus is an enclave of artists and illustrators who create drawings, some of which eventually become fabric. Because they've been doing this for more than 75 years, they might have, for example, 5,000 different polka dot designs spanning decades, some of which were chosen and manufactured at the time, and some of which were not.

Clients often came to them and requested designs similar to some examples, and they'd put their artists to work coming up with new options. Even though they had an enormous back catalog of drawings of fashion fabrics, they had no way to locate, say, some third-choice design from the 1970s that would probably be exactly what their customer wanted in 2020 because their warehouse contained thousands and thousands of files and fabric swatches organized by year.

Enter AI. The company sought to use AI to solve this

specific efficiency problem. They created a visual-based similarity search, which could identify designs from their back catalog that were visually similar to an example or even a specific aesthetic that their customer wanted. Suddenly, those 5,000 polka dot designs could be used again. They didn't always need to have their artists create new drawings for every customer request because they could give them ten options they already had on file. It was a far more efficient way of serving their clients.

IDENTIFY PROBLEMS AI SHOULD SOLVE

You may be familiar with the process of selecting and rolling out a software package—say, analytics software—for your entire company. Not only do you have to pick a winner from the many choices available, but you also have to deal with costs, training, and getting your team to accept the change. Managing all this, of course, requires some understanding ahead of time of what you're planning to do with the outputs of your new software. The benefits you think it will provide over time will drive how much time and money you're willing to spend getting it up and running.

In a lot of ways, AI is no different. You'll have to handle most of the same issues, and you'll be far more successful with a well-articulated plan that clearly describes the business problem you're attacking, the reasons AI is the right tool to solve it, and the outcomes you expect.

Walmart had a goal to increase repeat business by improving the customer experience of being in their stores. They decided that having fully stocked shelves was key to the in-store experience; if a customer goes looking for an item and it's out of stock, that's a negative experience they remember.

This problem seemed insurmountable. A given Walmart store stocks thousands of products on its shelves; having employees walk all the aisles four times a day, checking shelves against some spreadsheet of expected inventory was inefficient. In order to have up-to-date information, they'd have to hire a few dozen employees per store whose entire job would be documenting what was in or out of stock. Besides being expensive, these employees would clog up the aisles and crowd out the real customers.

Problems like these, which are tedious or repetitive for humans to solve, are often excellent opportunities for machine learning. If a task can only be done by repeating some actions over and over again, it's probably easy to teach it to a machine learning algorithm, whereas a human would hate the job and eventually burn out.

Walmart decided to automate the collection of this data. They partnered with Bossa Nova Robotics to build robots that would "walk" the aisles, taking huge panoramic images of the shelves. A machine learning model would analyze the images, identify the products on the shelves, and notice when they were missing. The system could then notify employees in the stockroom to refill out-of-stock items within minutes. The entire end-to-end process had to be completed in less than an hour for the data to be useful to Walmart employees.[18]

This data proved to be extremely useful. Not only were employees able to keep shelves stocked so a customer would never find a hole in the available inventory, they used the information to change the entire process of restocking shelves to do it much more efficiently. This is a great example of one big problem solved by many different small machine learning solutions alongside many hardware, software, and programmatic solutions. While ultimately Walmart disbanded the initiative,[19] deciding that the robots weren't sustainable forever and were proving to take up too much space in the aisles, the project scaled up considerably over a five-year period. Like most problems, machine learning is just one tool alongside many in the eventual best solution. Walmart is in no way unique in the way it solved this problem; similar problems

---

18   Linder, Courtney, "Bossa Nova Robotics raises $17.5 million in funding following Walmart announcement", *Pittsburgh Post-Gazette*, November 2017, https://www.post-gazette.com/business/tech-news/2017/11/14/Bossa-Nova-Robotics-receives-XXXXXXXX/stories/201711140008.

19   "Walmart Drops Bossa Nova Inventory Robotics Program - Highlights Retail Robotics Challenges & Opportunities." *Robotics Business Review*, 17 Nov. 2020, www.roboticsbusinessreview.com/opinion/walmart-drops-bossa-nova-inventory-robotics-program-highlights-retail-robotics-challenges-opportunities/.

that can be solved using machine learning as a piece of the solution can be found in nearly every industry.

For example, farmers have used machine learning very effectively to grow healthier food more sustainably without driving up costs.

Previously, farmers couldn't afford to hire the amount of manual labor it would require to selectively spray pesticides, so pesticides were simply sprayed everywhere—not ideal for the environment. Now, some farmers install cameras as part of their spraying system. A machine learning model does what the farmers can't: checks every leaf for bugs. It can then tell the sprayer exactly where to spray.[20] The farmers can buy, in some cases, 90% less of the pesticide they used to and reduce the amount that ends up on our produce.[21] Machine learning tools have also helped farms deploy a "search and destroy" strategy on encroaching weeds. Blue River Technologies®, an agriculture tech company that was acquired by John Deere®, uses cameras and machine learning to instantly tell the difference between the crop and the weeds and selectively target the weeds with herbicide. The business impact of these tech-

---

20 Strickler, Jordan. "Blue River Technology Uses Facebook AI For Weed Control." *Forbes*, Forbes Magazine, 7 Aug. 2020, www.forbes.com/sites/jordanstrickler/2020/08/07/facebook-ai-is-getting-into-agriculture/.

21 Simonite, Tom. "Why John Deere Just Spent $305 Million on a Lettuce-Farming Robot." *Wired*, Conde Nast, 7 Sept. 2017, www.wired.com/story/why-john-deere-just-spent-dollar305-million-on-a-lettuce-farming-robot.

nologies is massive. The farmers spend less on labor while using less pesticides and herbicides. It's a win-win for both the farmer's bottom line and the environment.

BUILD A CROSS-FUNCTIONAL TEAM

As a business leader, you might not be able to identify which problems are solvable with AI right away. You may not have the right data or context for that part of your organization. Perhaps you think, *"I'll just hire a data scientist, and they'll figure it out."* That's only a piece of the puzzle—there's much more to the solution than a single expert hire.

In order to be successful, you'll need to create a cross-functional team to identify the problems to attack and figure out how to solve them. In addition to data scientists, this team might include a user researcher to interview people who can provide candidate business problems to solve. It'll need a machine learning engineer who can figure out whether the data exists to solve the problem and how to get it.

Perhaps most importantly, this multidisciplinary team has to include a central role like a product manager or line-of-business owner who deeply understands the objectives being sought and who can make sure that the solution being developed will actually achieve the desired business outcome. The nontechnical components of a successful AI solution are just as important, if not more important, than the purely technical skills necessary to build a model.

Even with a wonderful business strategy, a well-articulated, specific problem, and a great team, it'll be impossible to achieve success without access to the data, tools, and infrastructure necessary to ingest each dataset, save it, move it to the right place, and manipulate it. The best-trained doctors can't perform surgery without a scalpel, an operating room, and a team of nurses and technicians to support them. So be sure your team includes operational folks who can speak to the intricacies and practical concerns of computing, storage, and network. Their support will be crucial to your strategy's success.

You'll also need to determine how you'll go about acquiring your data at the beginning of the process. Without reliable access to relevant, clean, high-quality data, all the hardware and infrastructure in the world won't be able to train and test a model. The owners of that data throughout your business are best equipped to provide context on its provenance and should be part of your team as well.

DEFINE WHAT SUCCESS LOOKS LIKE

Finally, it's vitally important to define success for your project up front. You'll need to be clear ahead of time about the metrics your solution will optimize. It's generally a good idea to measure the thing you care about rather than a side effect, or else you run the risk of Wilson's team at eBay accidentally impacting revenue with accessory pollution. If you want to optimize productivity, for example, don't measure the number of sick days your team is taking. If they get twice the amount done as another team while taking more sick days, you'll never know it. Make sure the thing you measure is the thing you want to measure.

Imagine a model that can detect brain cancer in the general public with 99 percent accuracy. On paper, that sounds incredible, right? But in reality, this model doesn't even have to be trained to meet this metric because, in the general public, the occurrence of brain cancer is less than one percent. A model that simply predicts, "No, you don't have brain cancer" every single time will be 99 percent accurate. A definition of success based on this metric alone wouldn't drive a brain cancer detection model that solves any significant problem.[22]

Some projects do care about metrics like accuracy, of course, but others, like the brain cancer model, care more about reducing false positives or false negatives. The nuances of difference between those metrics can be difficult for business people to understand sometimes—but

---

22 "Brain Tumor: Statistics." *Cancer.Net*, 12 Feb. 2020, https://www.cancer.net/cancer-types/brain-tumor/statistics.

it's critical to get your head around. Education during the strategy development is important so that everyone has the same understanding of what success means and the problems with achieving it.

LinkedIn® makes its money by charging companies seeking to hire people for access to likely candidates through their messaging system, InMail. User engagement with InMail is, therefore, an important metric for them and a leading indicator of business. They've used machine learning to increase that engagement in fairly narrow ways—for example, by extracting relevant information from job postings to provide targeted recommendations to likely applicants.[23]

With this strategy, LinkedIn has to be careful of the downstream effects of its models. Without a direct link between engagement and revenue, they run the risk of optimizing engagement to the exclusion of revenue or losing information about how a machine learning model is actually performing.

Everyone starts their AI projects with positive, forward-thinking objectives for their business, but far too many start implementation without clearly defining their strat-

---

23 Guo, Qi, "The AI Behind LinkedIn Recruiter search and recommendation systems", *LinkedIn Engineering*, April 2019, https://engineering.linkedin.com/blog/2019/04/ai-behind-linkedin-recruiter-search-and-recommendation-systems.

egy and metrics. Don't fall into the same trap. It's easy to spend a lot of money to build cool technology, but if it doesn't serve your business, your project will be a failure. Make sure you can clearly and specifically connect the dots between the output of your machine learning project and business value, or else you'll end up wasting a lot of time, money, and energy doing something you don't actually care about.

eBay took their planning incredibly seriously. They identified problems to solve, created and enabled a cross-functional team, and executed a multi-year strategy with great success. Even if your company isn't as large or doesn't have their resources, you can still take from their example the importance of developing a strategy up front.

However, make sure you don't try to do everything at once. If you try to solve all your business problems at the same time, you'll succeed at none of them. Start small, then iterate and expand the solution over time. The problem you choose to tackle first will set the stage for the rest of your AI journey.

CHAPTER 3

PICKING THE GOLDILOCKS PROBLEM

"Besides looking like a bunch of rampaging amateurs, leaders who try to shove AI approaches where they don't belong usually end up with solutions which are too costly to maintain in production. Instead, find a good problem to solve and may the best solution win. If you can do it without AI, so much the better. ML/AI is for those situations where the other approaches don't get you the performance you need."

—CASSIE KOZYRKOV, CHIEF DECISION
SCIENTIST, GOOGLE, INC.[24]

Building AI into your business doesn't have to mean leveraging machine learning to solve every problem all at once.

---

24 Kozyrkov, Cassie. "12 Steps to Applied AI." *Medium*, The Startup, 17 Nov. 2020, medium.com/swlh/12-steps-to-applied-ai-2fdad7fdcdf3.

In fact, it shouldn't. It's more important to pick the single right problem to start with and build momentum with its solution. That's called identifying the "Goldilocks problem."

Before the software company Autodesk® began tackling AI, its technical support services were decidedly analog. When the millions of engineers and architects who rely on AutoCAD LT® software to create technical designs and models needed assistance, their options were to call the helpline or send a help request via email. This built a lengthy queue that was managed manually. An average support case took over a day to resolve. So, when Autodesk decided to bring AI into the mix, they narrowed in on one preeminent issue: improving the customer experience by reducing case resolution time.[25] Rather than building a model to help automate all the inquiries into their contact center, which spanned dozens of use cases and questions, they focused on solving a single problem that represented a huge percentage of incoming support tickets: password resets.[26]

This focus—identifying a narrow problem that had business importance—was critical to its success.

25 "Speeding customer response times by 99 percent with IBM Watson", https://www.ibm.com/case-studies/autodesk-inc.

26 "Legal Notices & Trademarks." *Autodesk*, www.autodesk.com/company/legal-notices-trademarks/trademarks/guidelines-for-use.

Deciding which inbound inquiries were about resetting a password was a good task for natural language processing because people usually describe the problem in one of a handful of similar ways: "I need help logging in." "I want to reset my password." Autodesk had access to a huge volume of historical data—emails and voice recordings—of users asking them to solve this problem. Password-reset requests represented thousands of inquiries a month. If Autodesk could automate the process, they'd significantly free up their contact center resources to solve other customer problems more quickly.

Most importantly, the customers making these requests tended to get frustrated that something as simple as resetting a password took a day and a half to resolve. These were highly technical users unable to access one of the primary tools they needed to do their jobs. The poor customer experience was costing the company money.

With this specific goal identified, Autodesk built a model to recognize which incoming tickets were password-reset requests. If they could automatically identify these as soon as the inquiry was sent, they could then route that customer to a user interface able to reset a customer's password without having another human involved. The team didn't just have to build a natural language processing model to detect password reset inquiries. They also had to connect several internal systems to verify that the person requesting the reset had the authorization to do so. In the end, they were able to reduce the average time to resolve a password reset request drastically—from 1.5 days down to 10-15 minutes.

This solution was a fantastic proof of concept. Also, the natural language processing model, which did the heavy lifting of determining which inbound requests were about password resets, didn't need to be perfect to start adding value. Even if at the beginning, the model only successfully recognized 70 percent of the inbound password-reset requests, that still contributed meaningfully to the bottom line of reducing customer resolution time. Over time, the model improved and expanded its capabilities. Autodesk built up the model to recognize 60 distinct use cases, ranging from activation-code requests to address changes, contract problems, technical issues, and more. These 60 use cases were similarly easy to resolve and automate, freeing up their customer service agents to help customers with more complex issues and dropping their average case resolution time from 1.5 days to 5.4 minutes.

According to Gregg Spratto, Autodesk's VP of Operations at the time, "The solution's capability of recognizing the context of the question has resulted in Autodesk being able to resolve customer inquiries up to 99 percent faster." This translated directly into cost savings and a better customer experience and led to a larger investment in AI throughout the organization.

Autodesk set itself up for success by picking a manageable and valuable first problem to solve. Their problem was narrowly scoped but had a noticeable, measurable business impact. They didn't try to solve all 60 of the use cases they eventually automated at the beginning; the team focused on just one problem, solved it quickly and well, and proved their business value. At the same time, they built the prototype for all the solutions to come. Perhaps more importantly, the team didn't just build a model and throw it over the fence to someone else.

If you can solve the first problem you attack and prove the impact AI can have, you'll have a much easier time getting support and resources to tackle the next 10 problems. You'll likely identify a variety of potentially great first problems. Choosing the problem that hits the sweet spot of scale and impact with a manageable machine learning component is the most important thing you can do to set yourself up for success.

So what are the characteristics of this Goldilocks problem?

START SMALL

As we've discussed, the best Goldilocks problem is small

enough that you can solve it quickly. Problems that involve classifying something into one of two buckets—password-reset request, yes or no?—are great candidates. It's usually fairly easy for reasonable people to agree on these types of classifications; a single person can quickly make the yes-or-no decision, and that decision won't be questioned by others. In fact, there's a high degree of certainty that most others would draw the same conclusion. This makes it very obvious when you've been successful in solving the problem at scale.

By way of contrast, problems that require resolving ambiguity are probably not great candidates. If two people might disagree on the right answer, you'll have a much harder time showing that your model does the right thing most of the time. Whereas, imagine if the problem you choose is classifying each incoming ticket into one of 100 categories. It would take a well-trained person weeks to learn the categories and provide enough examples to get it right; even then, other people might agree or disagree frequently. This isn't a good Goldilocks problem. Another example: perhaps you're the owner of a hotel booking website, and you choose to solve the problem of categorizing customers' reviews. This requires tagging each review with tags that correspond to what they mention—amenities, food, location, price, etc. This tagging would likely be quickly agreed upon by most people, but the activity is incredibly resource-intensive.

Start simple. Start with something that a human can do reliably over and over again but that a computer could do at a scale and speed a human could not.

In 1965, the Postal Service put the first high-speed optical character reader (OCR) into operation that could handle a preliminary sort automatically.[27] Instead of humans sorting the mail into zip codes by looking at each piece manually, a machine could now recognize the zip code and do the work much faster. In 1982, the first computer-driven single-line optical character reader was employed, making the process even more efficient by way of a printed barcode that automated mail sorting from start to finish. Finally, in 1997, the USPS took it a step even further by contracting researchers to develop handwriting recognition technology; it was launched right before the Christmas mail rush and saved the Postal Service upwards of $90 million that first year in the field. This evolution is all centered around the same simple problem: looking at a line of information and putting the piece of mail where it needs to go. It's one narrow task that a human can do quickly and accurately

27   Saldarini, Katy. "Postal Service Tests Handwriting Recognition System." *Government Executive*, Government Executive, 17 Jan. 2012, https://www.govexec.com/federal-news/1999/02/postal-service-tests-handwriting-recognition-system/1746/. "Pioneers in AI Systems." *Center for Unified Biometrics and Sensors - University at Buffalo*, 20 Apr. 2020, https://www.buffalo.edu/cubs/research/pioneers-in-ai-systems.html. U.S. Postal Service is adopting AI tech to process package data faster By Michelai Graham / staff. "U.S. Postal Service Is Adopting AI Tech to Process Package Data Faster." *Technical.ly DC*, 12 Nov. 2019, https://technical.ly/dc/2019/11/12/united-states-postal-service-artificial-intelligence-technology-process-package-data-faster/.

but that a computer can do at a massively faster scale. It's a great solution to a Goldilocks problem.

GO WHERE THE DATA IS

Another characteristic of a good Goldilocks problem is a large bank of historical data obtained through past instances of solving that same problem. Autodesk's password-reset inquiries fit this bill: the company had a pool of past instances of password-reset inquiries and the corresponding answers from human agents correctly identifying the nature of the inquiry. All past cases that have been classified into buckets become training data for your model. If you don't have examples that have already been categorized, you might still have examples that you could spend time having humans go through and categorize now—time-consuming work, but of huge benefit to your project.

It's also important to ensure that the data you have wouldn't introduce bias or unfairness unintentionally. A customer at IBM was using speech recognition in a US call center that primarily served Spanish speakers. The customer was dissatisfied with the accuracy they were getting; their system wasn't able to identify requests reliably. When they came to IBM, the team knew immediately what the problem was and how it could be solved; unfortunately, they didn't have the data to do it. They needed a significant amount of call center data that had originated from a similar industry and similar accents—Spanish in the US varies a lot acoustically, based on where the speaker learned it. The model the team had deployed for this customer had mostly been trained on Chilean Spanish, which didn't represent a large percentage of the Spanish spoken in this call center. It wasn't a good Goldilocks problem. Even though the classifications were reasonably simple, the team didn't have enough data of the right kind to solve the problem for a general audience.

This is fairly common when a team tries to take an off-the-shelf model and apply it to a new and different use case. It's unusual when the off-the-shelf model can be applied successfully to a purpose for which it was not intended. The Spanish language speech recognition model was "good" by many measures, but just not by the measure that this particular company cared about for this particular business purpose. They needed to adapt and fine-tune the model for their particular use case. This is a great opportunity to deploy transfer learning—when you start with a base model fairly close to what you need and then fine-tune it with more specific and granular data to be exactly what you need, in this case, specific jargon that was going to be used in this call center.

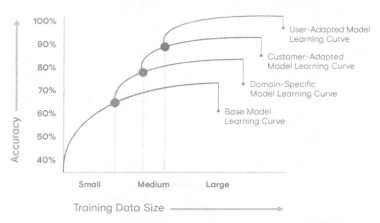

Comparative Efficacy of Learning Curve Models

User-Adapted Model Learning Curve

Customer-Adapted Model Learning Curve

Domain-Specific Model Learning Curve

Base Model Learning Curve

Accuracy

100%
90%
80%
70%
60%
50%
40%

Small   Medium   Large

Training Data Size

Learning Curves: As the domain narrows, learning accelerates from Rama Akkiraju[28]

Another example: if Autodesk's backlog of examples had not primarily been in English, they would have needed to make sure that they identified the language of incoming requests first before attempting to classify them using their model, or else they'd adversely impact customers who were making requests in Spanish if previously the customer service agents understood Spanish and responded accordingly. It's important to have a clear idea of the boundaries of your problem you are and are not solving for—and be able to communicate and be transparent about those boundaries.

---

28   Akkiraju, Rama. "Artificial Intelligence (AI) Service and Solution Development Methodology for Enterprises - Part 3." *Medium*, Medium, 17 June 2018, medium.com/@rama.akkiraju/ artificial-intelligence-ai-service-and-solution-development-methodology-for-enterprises-part-2-2d48a97e8855.

DELIVER QUICK WINS

In some cases, you'll have a use case that can be solved in part or whole by an off-the-shelf model. An off-the-shelf model is one that someone else has already developed and is selling as a service. This means that the model comes pre-trained, and the data that it's trained on matches the specific problem you're solving. A common off-the-shelf model currently available, for example, is one that takes incoming customer requests and quickly recognizes what language the request is in. If you can deliver value quickly, and you don't need to build a custom machine learning model to do so, then great! Choose that. The business will be far more willing to tolerate the nine to 12 months it can take to get a more complex, custom model built, tested, and in production. When trying to pick this first problem, you should definitely consult with the data scientists and other members of the team to see if there are opportunities to take this kind of shortcut.

Additionally, off-the-shelf training datasets offer a quick, cost-effective alternative to collecting and annotating data from scratch and can be used even if you're building your own model. High-quality datasets can be used as-is or customized for specific project types. Companies that offer these datasets guarantee accuracy up front, removing variability out of the model training process. Not only is it advantageous from a price and speed perspective, but growing requirements for data privacy and security from both customers and authorities can make it complicated to use data you have on hand.

MAKE AN IMPACT

Although it should be small enough to be solved quickly, a Goldilocks problem should still be big enough to have a clear business impact. It's easy to see the value of a solution that measurably increases revenue or decreases costs. If your solution frees up people from performing a fairly mundane or tedious task that doesn't give them a lot of satisfaction—like, for instance, sorting individual envelopes by reading zip codes over and over, it'll be seen positively and reduce costs. A good rule of thumb is to not only be clear on the business impact but be able to clearly measure and prove it. The Autodesk password reset fit this goal perfectly. They were able to quantify in time, and customer satisfaction scored the benefit of more quickly solving password reset issues. Often, Goldilocks problems are linked to obvious things like revenue, customer net promoter score (NPS), or time value.

It's also helpful for the first solution to be novel or innovative in some way, to grab even more attention. If non-AI teams get excited about what the AI team can do, the whole organization will start coming up with problems to solve and give support to the AI team who works on them.

FOCUS ON THE ROI

The organizational maturity of your company—the amount of experience with AI and the degree to which it trusts data to help it make decisions—will help you determine the Goldilocks problem you pick. Some organizations have no trust in data at all. Others may think it isn't important or helpful or may avoid using it unless it supports the opinions they already have. And then you have more personal concerns; AI models change internal power structures and can (and will) eliminate jobs. Resistance to this kind of change often looks like an insistence by those affected that the model "will never work." Demonstrating the value of AI with an easy win can go a long way toward helping organizations like this mature into data-driven companies that trust data to help them make decisions, and as a result, are willing to use AI to tackle larger problems.

More practically, companies that don't have a lot of experience with AI will need to start with something easy before moving on to harder problems. Nobody will do it perfectly the first time, so it's helpful to start with a problem that, if it doesn't go quite right, won't cause major harm or embarrassment to the business. Again, Autodesk's Goldilocks problem is a great example of this concept. If the NLP classifier didn't work at peak accuracy and multitudes of password reset inquiries were misclassified, it would certainly be inconvenient but not hugely detrimental. The AI team, and the company as a whole, needs the freedom and safety to learn how to apply the technologies appropriately before graduating to more mainstream business processes or riskier parts of the organizations.

For whatever problem you choose, you should be able to calculate a baseline describing how you're performing today. Without that, you won't be able to determine the return on investment your solution will provide. It can be hard to delay digging into the data to see what's there, but it's very important to give realistic expectations up front.

If the business units assume that they'll pass you data and you'll deliver magical insight, they'll usually be disappointed. If your project fails, buyer's remorse will set in, and it'll be a while before they invest in an AI solution again.

For example, imagine that a large tech company once contracted with a company to build a better car alarm. This company claimed that everyone ignored their car alarms because they were inaccurate—and ignoring a car alarm, of course, makes it useless. If they could make the triggering of the alarm more accurate, they believed, more people would pay attention to them because they'd have a greater expectation that something was actually wrong.

The large tech company was, at this point, fairly experienced at bringing AI projects into the world. A standard part of their process was to begin with a design workshop in order to make sure the right problem was being addressed before spending money and effort building a model. During this workshop, while they were trying to identify the exact pain point, the designer in the room realized that this wasn't a machine learning problem but a design problem. Even if you know your car alarm is triggered with 99.999 percent accuracy, the first time an alarm goes off that isn't yours, you're going to forget it. The second time, you'll question whether you should even look; chances are it isn't yours, anyway. The third time, it's the car alarm that cried wolf, and the alarm is officially useless.

Instead of making the alarm more accurate, it needed to be personalized, like a ring tone, so you'd be able to identify your alarm from everyone else's and know you really needed to pay attention. By workshopping the problem before beginning model development, the company saved themselves a bunch of time, and the car alarm company a lot of money and disappointment.

Cassie Kozyrkov, Chief Decision Scientist at Google, underscores this point. "Besides looking like a bunch of rampaging amateurs, leaders who try to shove AI approaches where they don't belong usually end up with solutions which are too costly to maintain in production.

Instead, find a good problem to solve and may the best solution win. If you can do it without AI, so much the better. ML/AI is for those situations where the other approaches don't get you the performance you need."[29]

The most AI-mature companies have gone beyond being merely data-driven. Because of their many past successes with AI, they use it religiously. Every model is rigorously A/B tested. Financial decisions are made entirely based on data. Discussions may begin by comparing differing opinions but always come back to identifying the right decision based on the data supporting that position. AI can really take off in companies like this; they have the culture and the processes in place to implement AI quickly whenever they identify a new use for it.

Evaluate the level of experience within your company before you settle on a problem. Choose a quickly solvable problem with an easily understandable impact in order to build momentum with demonstrated success. You're likely to have a variety of problems that are good candidates for your Goldilocks problem, but when starting out, progress is far more important than perfection, so pick what seems to be a good first problem and just start.

Even though Autodesk began with the lofty goal of reduc-

---

29 Kozyrkov, Cassie. "12 Steps to Applied AI." *Medium*, The Startup, 17 Nov. 2020, https://medium.com/swlh/12-steps-to-applied-ai-2fdad7fdcdf3.

ing case resolution times, they wisely started with a single small problem, solved it quickly and well, and gained the trust and acceptance within the company to start expanding their AI model to improve things even further. Had they tried to solve the 60 use cases they knew of up front, they'd likely have failed to do any of them very well, and the entire project might have died on the vine. Thanks to their excellent choice of a Goldilocks problem, they helped their entire company mature in its use of data.

As we mentioned earlier, your solution to that Goldilocks problem will be materially affected by the data you have available. The data you have available and how you prepare it will have a huge impact on your success. In the next chapter, we'll discuss the kinds and quality of the data you'll need, as well as how to get it.

CHAPTER 4

DO YOU HAVE THE RIGHT DATA?

"Unfortunately, we have biases that live in our data, and if we don't acknowledge that and if we don't take specific actions to address it, then we're just going to continue to perpetuate them or even make them worse."

—KATHY BAXTER, PRINCIPAL ARCHITECT,
ETHICAL AI PRACTICE, SALESFORCE®

Andrej Karpathy, Director of AI and Autopilot Vision at Tesla®, gave a presentation at Appen's (formerly Figure Eight's) Train AI Summit in 2018 that highlighted a fundamental but undervalued truth: when creating AI in the real world, the data used to train the model is far more important than the model itself. This is a reversal of the typical paradigm represented by academia, where data science PhDs spend most of their focus and effort on creating new models. But the data used to train models in academia are only meant to prove the functionality of the model, not solve real problems. To put a model into production and achieve real business objectives, it must be trained with the right data. Out in the real world, high-quality and accurate data that can be used to train a working model is incredibly tricky to collect.

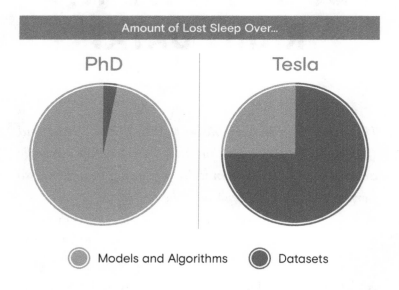

One of the harder AI problems being worked on right now, and where Andrej Karpathy has leading experience, is the creation of a self-driving car. A self-driving car has to be taught not just how to navigate from point A to point B, but how to recognize and interpret its entire environment. It needs to identify obstacles, determine its distance from each of them, and decide how to navigate the space they both inhabit. Accuracy is absolutely essential; if the car makes the wrong decision or misidentifies an obstacle, lives could be lost.

Perhaps the first and most important obstacle a car should be taught to recognize and avoid is a pedestrian. But teaching a model to recognize a pedestrian in sensor data— say, a 2D image—can be extremely difficult. At first, the problem seems simple: annotate your dataset by drawing boxes around pedestrians in each image, and the model will learn what they look like.

But complications emerge rapidly. What if a pedestrian is in a wheelchair? What about a baby carriage? What about the reflection of a person in a windshield or mirror? What about a poster at a bus stop with a picture of a person on it? These cases are actually a lot less rare than you might think.

You have to communicate all of these possibilities and how to handle them to the annotators of your data. If you aren't clear about how each of these deviations should be treated, then they'll be labeled inconsistently, and the model will have a very difficult time figuring out how to treat those situations when they come up.

THE RIGHT DATA

Once you've clarified the Goldilocks problem you're going to solve, it should be fairly straightforward to identify the data you need in order to solve it. The data science team can help shake out the details, but the problem itself will dictate the qualities of the data you'll need. For the self-driving car, data required might include items like stoplight colors, turning signals on or off, hand signals from bicyclists, and so on.

Once you have identified the necessary data, the problem becomes acquiring that data. Review any data you already possess for accuracy and annotation. Then, locate a source from which to acquire the rest of the data you'll need. Guaranteeing that you'll be able to secure a steady source of high-quality, annotated data for the duration of the model's existence is a fundamental prerequisite to the project. If you don't have the right data, your project will fail in any number of ways.

Walmart had no data at all when they started their shelf-inventorying robot project. Before beginning to build the model, they had to gather enough data to start with, having robots go up and down the aisles in dozens of stores, collecting images.

Once they had images, their next challenge was annotating the data. A supervised model can't work with raw, binary image data. It has to be told what each image means at first in order to be trained. To accomplish this, Walmart split the annotation workflow into four stages.

In the first stage, a team simply identified the breaks between shelving units within each panoramic image and annotated the image data with their locations. This would be used to train the stage of the model processing pipeline responsible for splitting an image into those shelving units. For the second stage, the team took the shelving unit images and annotated the borders of the individual shelves. In the third stage, the team identified the parts of each shelf image that represented product labels or UPCs, and in the fourth stage, they annotated the label images with transcriptions of those labels.

All of this annotation had to be performed by humans until enough annotated data had been amassed to train a model that could break down a panoramic image of an entire aisle into text representations of each individual label. The annotation itself wasn't particularly tricky work, but it had to be done at high volume, with high accuracy, and in a matter of minutes. Without a process in place that guaranteed the ongoing availability of annotated data, Walmart couldn't be confident that they'd be able to build and maintain a model long-term.

When you first start identifying the data you'll use for your model, you'll want to factor in how available it is. Do you have it? How easy is it to access? How much does it cost? Has the data already been prepared or manipulated in some way? Do you understand what's in it? Is it representative of edge cases? Will you be able to access more data like it in the future?

Alyssa

If the data you need is only available for a short time, you might need to locate another source. While I was at IBM, one of the teams was using training data we got through a business relationship with a social media platform for a model using data. When the contract between the two companies ended, however, we were cut off from using that data and obligated to delete all the data we still had. Since we'd trained all our models from that source, we had to dump them and start over with a different dataset we would have long-term access to. In retrospect, we should never have set ourselves up to depend on that data in the first place since we could have predicted that it wouldn't be available forever. This is a surprisingly common problem. Earlier, we discussed how a machine learning expert ran into this with a health tracking app. At one point, he scraped data off of another company's website just to find out later the business had changed directions, and he was no longer allowed to use that data. Ensuring the model-building team has the right data is very much a problem for the business folks involved.

Depending on the problem you're solving, you may be able to create data you're missing. For example, if you're optimizing workflows on a web application, you can have the application track user interactions and clicks. In some other cases, you may be able to change the process so that the data you need is created as a side effect of normal operations. Even if you don't have a dataset ready-made to train your model, you can often still find a way to get what you need and guarantee a source for that data in the future. And if you're starting from scratch, you don't have to do it all yourself; companies exist specifically to partner with you on your data needs. You can find one of these expert partners to help you. Sourcing the right data can be costly, but it's more than well worth the money, and if you've picked a good Goldilocks problem, advocating for the funds to source the right data to solve the problem shouldn't be exceedingly difficult. This is a good litmus test for the impact of your business problem.

IT DOESN'T END THERE

Don't forget to allocate resources for the ongoing training of your model. Models have to be trained continually, or they'll become less accurate over time as the real world changes around them (this is called "model drift" and is talked about in chapter 9). It's vital you ensure your data will be available on an ongoing basis. An industry analyst recently asked, "Don't you think that, in five years, the need for so much training data will go away because all these models will have been trained already? I find it hard to believe that some of your customers would create new training data for the exact same use case for five years in a row." We believe he couldn't be more wrong. Not only is this done, but it's also extremely common.

Big companies like Amazon, Google, and Apple employ some of the world's best machine learning scientists and arguably possess some of the world's best technology in the space. They also have access to inexhaustible sources of high-quality data. Even with all of this, they spend hundreds of millions of dollars every year annotating data to achieve content moderation to make sure that it keeps up to date with the evolving semantics of language. The taboos of today are different from those of years ago when their models were first created; without constantly re-annotating and retraining their models, they would let more and more explicit content through as public opinions and standards changed.

When the team building Walmart's inventory-tracking model finally achieved the accuracy they needed, they learned that Walmart was rolling out a cosmetic change to the design of many of their product labels. This meant all the training data they'd been collecting for one of the models around label identification didn't match what would be encountered in production, and the accuracy of the model dropped substantially.

Luckily, because they continually had robots roll down the aisles and take pictures, they could control the source of the data. They also didn't necessarily need to throw out all the training data. Potentially, the new design of the labels would be similar enough to the old design that, although the model wouldn't be as accurate as it was, it could still get close. The labels would still probably be written in English, and the bar codes would still be black on a white background. Nevertheless, it's important to refresh the model with new data to keep it up to date and give it the refinement to handle the new reality. Your data is only as good as it is at the point in time it's collected.

WHERE DID THE DATA COME FROM?

It's also important to consider the provenance of your data. It's incredibly common in an enterprise to find data scattered throughout databases in different departments without any documentation about where it's from or how it got there. As data makes its way from the point where it's collected into the database where you find it, it's very likely that it has been changed or manipulated in a meaningful way. If you make assumptions about how the data you're using got there, you could end up producing a useless model.

Let's say you're building a model to help categorize and optimize employee expenses, so you get access to your company's expense system. That seems like everything you need—it's got pictures of receipts, and it's been at least partially annotated with the amounts and business purposes for each line item. A more junior data science team might just take that data and run with it. But they wouldn't know that the policy in the department is different for expenses over $100; those requests skip the normal system and go directly to someone's desk for approval.

In this scenario, the team would burn a lot of time and money building a model they couldn't use. Because they would have made assumptions about the provenance of the data, the model they'd produce wouldn't solve the business problem. Instead, they should have made sure they knew that the raw data wasn't changed on its way to their datastore and also that their dataset represented all of the raw data, rather than just a part.

When Walmart first began their project, they only had data from a single store, just enough to get started experimenting. When they expanded to include a total of five stores, their model didn't perform very well—not that they expected it to, at this stage. Although the five stores were essentially similar, they had slightly different layouts, slightly different looks and feels, and occasionally different products on their shelves. The model that trained on just one store lacked coverage of the data that represented all the inputs it would encounter in production. Far from an isolated incident, this kind of problem is incredibly common. Product managers should expect it and plan for it.

Ensuring that the training data examples cover all the use cases that will happen in the production deployment is absolutely required for a model to perform. You have to make sure that you don't artificially limit what your model can handle because you haven't thought through all of the use cases your users will have. Of course, you can't know what you don't know, but you have to try to anticipate what will happen in a real production environment. Don't trust your assumptions—verify them based on the data you have access to, and ensure you monitor the models in production to identify edge cases.

The data scientist working on a model is often many steps removed from the day-to-day customer activity that they're trying to create a model for, so when the project is kicking off, take the opportunity to get up close and personal with the business problem you're solving—akin to when Bossa Nova sent its data science team members into Walmart stores to walk the aisles. Have some user researchers explore the problem before you start to make sure that you really understand what's happening. Ask people who are actually working in the area about the characteristics of your training data to see how it differs from reality.

DATA QUALITY

As you evaluate whether your data covers your use cases, make sure you take into account the quality of that data. As Walmart increased the number of stores they gathered data from, they also encountered a corresponding rise in errors in that data—a robot went down the wrong aisle, or a power loss resulted in missing runs. Data that's bad or just irrelevant has to be detected and cleaned out. Annotating it would just result in a poorly trained model. But as that data is cleaned out, you'll have to make sure that you weren't counting on the bad data for coverage, or you'll be back where you started.

Data quality also depends on the accuracy of its annotations. To some extent, you'll want to have quality control processes verifying that the people annotating the data do so completely and correctly, or the accuracy of your model will suffer. For example, if you're annotating images by drawing boxes around the cars in the picture, it will matter a lot if you draw the box too big, including a lot of things that are not a car. The model will take a lot longer to learn what a car looks like if you tell it that tree branches or roads are cars. Similarly, if data annotation consists of transcribing voice messages, transcribing the file incorrectly—say, excluding a word, including words not there, or getting words wrong—will result in a poor model. It's not the model's fault; you will have trained it on incorrect data. Garbage in, garbage out.

A recent real-world example of the need for high-quality data arose in the COVID-19 pandemic. Health organizations around the world found themselves hamstrung in delivering necessary health and safety guidelines to populations of people whose native languages are under-resourced in language technology. Appen joined with other large data companies like Amazon, Facebook, Google, and Microsoft to work with Translators without Borders® on sourcing and annotating data for 37 under-resourced languages.[30] The initiative is developing datasets of 70,000 key COVID-19 terms, translated and accessible in Translators without Borders' online language data portal with the intent of informing future machine learning projects.

Humans aren't always the ones annotating data. In some cases, you can use machine learning models to annotate or augment data in order to use it in another machine learning model. You can use an object detection model to annotate all the cars from the picture first, then ask human annotators to review that annotation, make adjustments on the bounding boxes, or add missed bounding boxes. Or you can use an automatic speech recognition (ASR) model to transcribe voice data to text first, then get a human annotator to review and adjust the transcription results. There are some problems with this approach, such

30 Communications, TWB. "TWB Partners with Tech Leaders to Develop COVID-19 Language Technology." *Translators without Borders*, 6 July 2020, https://translatorswithoutborders.org/TICO-19-announcement.

as the biases of the model producing the annotations can end up influencing the model trained on the result, so a human will still have to review and correct the data before it can be used. Nevertheless, if you can make it work for your specific use case, you can potentially save a lot of the expense of human annotation.

At the beginning of your AI journey, justifying your costs will almost certainly be one of your primary focuses, but try to avoid using cheaper sources of data at the expense of quality. Sure, using cheaper data will save money up front, but as a result, building and refining the model will take considerably more time—and the cost of data scientists far outweighs the initial cost of good data. You'll be much better served in terms of both time and cost by sparing no expense on high-quality data at the outset. A recent Gartner Data Quality Market Survey estimated that data quality issues impact businesses to the tune of approximately $15 million lost in 2017.[31]

DATA SECURITY

As you pull together data to feed your project, you'll almost certainly have to address how you handle security. There are obvious cases, such as when you're using personally identifiable data, medical data, or government-controlled

31 "How to Stop Data Quality Undermining Your Business." *Smarter With Gartner*, https://www.gartner.com/smarterwithgartner/how-to-stop-data-quality-undermining-your-business/.

data, where your usage will be limited by contractual or legal obligation.

Naturally, controlling access to these datasets will have to be factored into your data acquisition strategy.

Other datasets, while not explicitly sensitive, may still need to be handled securely; it depends on the context of who has it and why. User likes on Facebook, while maybe not individually sensitive, still represent important business intelligence considered en masse. Even if the data is anonymized so no personally identifiable information could leak out, if it got into the wrong hands, it could be catastrophic for Facebook because they use that information to build their algorithms, and in some cases, sell it directly to advertisers.

A large tech manufacturer was working on a very sensitive project that required them to annotate coughs they detected through microphones on the devices they sold. They asked the annotators to mark where the coughs occurred, whether it was a wet cough or a dry cough, and so on. Now, nothing identified the audio as belonging to any particular person, but they still handled the data with extreme sensitivity. For one thing, if The New York Times had published a story saying, "Tech companies are recording your cough off of your device!" it would have creeped people out and created a lot of bad press. Besides that, it could have alerted their competitors to what they were doing, even if the only sources of their cough data were internal to the company.

Walmart made sure when setting up its data pipeline that the data from its inventory robots went to a secure platform and that all the annotators had signed confidentiality agreements. While anyone could go into a Walmart and start writing down all the products on the shelves, the layout of the stores and the placement of items considered at scale across many stores constitute valuable business information. They can't have just anyone review it without potentially giving away a competitive advantage.

The US Department of Veterans Affairs, aiming to reduce the number of veterans who commit suicide, uses AI to predict when a veteran is at risk for suicide through its REACH VET program.[32] The team built a model based on medical record data, use of VA services, and medication information to determine each tracked veteran's risk of suicide. This model relies on extremely sensitive information, and it is critically important these data remain secure. Because this model included medical information, the data collection also had to be HIPAA compliant.

---

32 Carey, Benedict. "Can an Algorithm Prevent Suicide?" *The New York Times*, The New York Times, 23 Nov. 2020, www.nytimes.com/2020/11/23/health/artificial-intelligence-veterans-suicide. html; "We're Here Anytime, Day or Night - 24/7." *Crisis Prevention*, www.research.va.gov/currents/0918-Study-evaluates-VA-program-that-identifies-Vets-at-highest-risk-for-suicide.cfm.

PULLING THE PIECES TOGETHER

All of these concerns—availability, coverage, provenance, quality, security—will need to be considered as you develop your data pipeline. Every step of the pipeline will need to be consistent, repeatable, and accurate. A well-thought-out, well-documented, repeatable pipeline will go a long way toward the success of the model in production long-term.

Those new to AI commonly believe that the hard part is building the model. In practice, however, data preparation and the building of the pipeline is very often a much bigger investment of time, resources, energy, and skillsets. Without a repeatable and scalable pipeline, the best-designed model won't be able to be used in production long enough to be useful. Data isn't a problem you can solve once and be done with. You'll have to get your data pipeline up and running and keep feeding it data for as long as your model is in production.

Once you're satisfied that you'll be able to sort out getting the right data to train your machine learning system, you'll need to start building the teams that will actually do it.

CHAPTER 5

DO YOU HAVE THE RIGHT ORGANIZATION?

"Great teamwork is the only way we create the breakthroughs that define our careers."

—PAT RILEY, PRESIDENT OF THE MIAMI HEAT

Alyssa

At the Watson division of IBM, we had the technical infrastructure and talented teams in place to build sophisticated models relatively quickly. But across all the teams I worked with, sourcing enough annotated data remained a significant headache. Part of my responsibilities included buying data from several different data annotation companies, but the number of places that had high volumes of high-quality data with the specificity and diversity required was quite small.

Even when I could find the data, it was extremely expensive.

I eventually left IBM to solve my own problem. I joined a data annotation company called CrowdFlower® (later known as Figure Eight Technologies) as VP of Product. They had a ton of data, but at the time, no machine learning intelligence to make that process more efficient. I had the privilege of being asked to help build a product to solve my own problem. I moved from a data-poor environment with highly skilled machine learning teams to a data-rich environment with teams that had little machine learning experience.

When I started, we had an engineering team, a machine learning team, and a product design team—and none of these teams talked to each other on a regular basis. Instead, each individual team had its own leadership, communication, and projects. They'd each have weekly meetings and report up the chain. There was very little cross-functional communication.

One of the outcomes of this vertical structure was that the organization as a whole didn't ship much software. Because they were on different schedules, the front-end team could build an entire UI before the back-end team got to their part of the project. When they finally caught up, the front-end team had moved on to something else, so connecting the front end to the back end didn't work very well. Meanwhile, the machine learning team had built a model, but no one was ready to accept it and integrate it into a product.

Even though we had a lot of smart and talented people on every team—the teams were siloed. In particular, the machine learning team, siloed away from the rest of the business, was without good instructions about the problems they should be solving. They got frustrated because they felt like they were working on things the business didn't care about. The product people were frustrated because they felt like they never got anything valuable out of the very expensive, high-paid, talented machine learning team.

In a startup, it's critical to differentiate and ship value often. As executives, we were concerned that if we didn't ship a high-value, machine learning based annotation product soon, we'd be out of business.

A few months later, with a new leadership team in place, we collaborated to solve the structural problem. Instead of only having a vertically oriented structure, we created an additional horizontal, functional team structure aligned around business investment areas. A team assigned to a business problem might consist of one product person, one designer, a few front-end developers, a couple of back-end developers, and a machine learning person. Each team would meet every day to coordinate and surface blockers. We didn't change any HR lines or any formal reporting structure; we just introduced a new concept of teams, which essentially meant that everyone was now part of two teams. There was the functional team: "product" or "machine learning" or "engineering," but now there was also a new horizontal team like "marketplace" or "enterprise." We encouraged these new horizontal teams to create an identity and fun name. The team responsible for enterprise features, such as security and analytics, adopted a Star Trek theme, calling themselves "Starship Enterprise." It was something that people could have fun with.

This change was met with considerable angst. The machine learning team claimed they couldn't possibly work in Agile. The front-end team argued they needed to stay together to build consistent front ends. Everyone was very resistant because it was a fundamentally different way of working than they were used to.

We counterbalanced it by pointing out that, although we were placing a much heavier emphasis on horizontal collaboration and Agile, they would still be part of their functional teams. The front-end developers would still meet weekly to help one another, which helped keep front-end development consistent across products, and the product teams would still meet to discuss product needs. But we placed a much heavier emphasis on horizontal collaboration.

We asked the team to stick with it, just for two weeks at a time. Every two weeks, we'd ask them what worked and didn't work, and we'd make changes in response to that feedback. Sometimes that meant moving one person from one team to another. Sometimes it meant changing the format of a meeting, or adding a new meeting, or getting rid of a meeting.

After six or seven iterations of this process, it started to really work. People had developed identities as members of these cross-functional teams. The annotation marketplace team identified with the problem they were solving and were proud of how their work empowered the business. The enterprise team was focused on security, scale, and heavy platform infrastructure. Each team developed its own identity and energy, and the team members developed a sense of belonging, which helped retention. We spent $100 to order stickers with team names and logos on them; soon, everyone in the company wanted stickers for their laptops (even those outside of technology). It became "cool" to be on one of these newly created horizontal teams. (Remember, from an HR perspective, these weren't formal "teams" at all, they were just ways of working).

Importantly, one big thing we did evaluate and change from an HR perspective was incentives. Historically, the product team would get a bonus based on products they shipped that generated revenue. The infrastructure team's bonus would be based on platform uptime. The QA team's bonus would depend on the bugs they kept out of production releases. The machine learning team's bonus would be pegged to the accuracy of their models.

Because these incentives weren't aligned, the functional teams weren't working toward the same goals. The machine learning team would toil away making models that were more and more accurate, which required expensive computers to retrain and run tests—but they weren't necessarily models that generated any revenue. The infrastructure team would resist rolling out new features or products because that risk would affect uptime.

When we restructured the teams, we restructured the incentives. We reduced the amount the functional goals contributed to their overall bonus to something closer to 30 percent and replaced the rest with a common incentive shared by all members of a team, top-line company revenue. That led to much more collaborative behavior and higher-quality, business-focused outcomes for the company.

All of these changes made us launch more product features

that customers cared about. The year before restructuring, we shipped three or four product enhancements. The year after, we shipped 33. All of this with basically the exact same people and resources. Not only were we putting products on the market, many of them included machine learning components because the machine learning people were embedded in each team.

It's incredibly common to be in the situation we started with. A company wants to make a big impact with AI, so they hire some data scientists and put them on their own team. But a business problem that can be solved by a model alone is very unusual. Most problems are multifaceted and require an assortment of skills—data pipelines, infrastructure, UX, business risk analysis. Put another way, machine learning is only useful when it's incorporated into a business process, customer experience or product, and actually gets released.

Machine learning products can't be developed by a team of data scientists alone. They require a team effort, and you need the team to work for the AI to work.

STRUCTURE

There's no one right way to organize your teams. In fact, there are many ways, and the one you choose will depend on where you are on your AI journey, your AI readiness, the sophistication of your team, the amount of talent you have, what your business objectives are, and how you measure success.

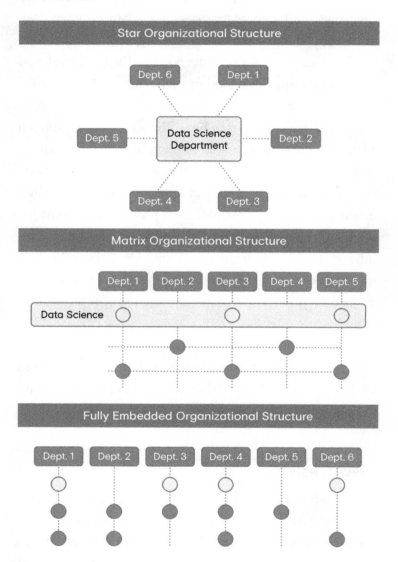

A "star" organizational structure may be the right choice for smaller companies or companies who've just started their AI journey and can't yet afford to build out AI throughout the organization. Instead, they'll create a centralized AI team—basically, a center of excellence—who will be in charge of AI efforts for the whole organization. They'll work with all the different domains and departments, and anyone with any AI needs will come to this team to get their model or application built.

A star shape is reasonably flexible. Its centralization allows AI efforts across the company to stay aligned, and it simplifies the allocation of limited resources. But once AI ramps up at the company, it'll be very difficult for a star-shaped AI organization to scale up to meet demand.

A "matrix" structure is more appropriate for bigger companies with more AI maturity. They might have quite a few AI problems they want to attack, in different domains or across product lines. For example, a company in the travel industry might have a hotel product line, a flights product line, and a vacations product line. All these product lines have different needs, but the AI problems they need to solve probably have a lot of similarities.

In a matrix-structured organization, the AI team members would be dedicated to these individual problems—two to three people working on the "hotels" product, a few on the "flights" product, and so on. Each subset would focus very closely on their business problem, working directly with the people from that domain to map their problem into machine learning, provide a solution, work with the product team to get it deployed to production, and even handle the customer feedback. Meanwhile, all these team members maintain their horizontal organization as part of the AI team, sharing ideas, learning new techniques, and comparing their domain-specific solutions to see how they can work together better.

A matrix organization structure can be very versatile, handling many problems across business domains simultaneously while allowing the right people to be brought to each one. Because each team member reports to managers in two dimensions, however, this structure can get extraordinarily complex as the number of individual problems grows. Managers in a matrix organization have to be very careful to make sure that responsibilities are clear, so the AI team members don't feel they have to serve competing loyalties.

The largest and most mature companies can move to a fully embedded AI structure. These companies will have used AI for a long time; it might be a core piece of some or all of their products. Every individual department will have its own data scientists and engineers who are able to build and deploy models on their own without reporting into a central organization. The machine learning team is just part of the domain team, and all the problems they work on are for that domain.

When every domain has its own AI team working more or less independently, coordination problems can develop. There's no reason not to maintain a level of horizontal communication between AI teams, similar to a matrix shape, to keep things consistent across the company.

MEMBERS

Breaking out Figure Eight's teams didn't all go perfectly. Many teams had gaps—for example, there weren't enough front-end people to staff every single team at a high enough level. Those gaps had to be filled with hiring. Depending on where you are as an organization, you may not have the ability to restructure quite as universally as Figure Eight did. But don't worry; even if you're starting completely from scratch, you can still build the team you need.

Almost always, the first person you'll want to hire or embed is someone who can deeply understand the business problem, such as a product manager or business analyst. This person wants to solve the problem using technology but can stay focused on the ROI, not pure solution success. This is typically someone who can be in control of the team's plan and guide it to create value. It's important that this not be a part-time role or filled by a contractor; this person should be fully invested in the team. That way, they can advocate for the project within the company. They can also efficiently guide the team to their goal without distraction or competing influence.

The next person to bring on board is a data scientist who can work with the product manager to map the business problem and objective onto a machine learning problem-solving framework. From there, you'll bring in a machine learning engineer.

Of course, your team isn't complete with only data scientists and machine learning engineers. There's a big gap between the academic approach of applied AI—building, testing, optimizing a model—and operationalizing its results. You'll want to include DevOps people on your team, who can manage the tooling that will allow you to operationalize, deploy, and maintain your models. This will allow your data scientists, who might not have a lot of experience operationalizing models on an enterprise-scale, to bring the best of their skills to bear on your problem.

If you build a model, it'll have to fit into your products or processes somehow, so you'll need the involvement of both architects and the owners of the systems you'll be integrating with. If you're building an application, you'll need a UI designer and an application developer.

One large fitness company tried implementing a health-care application using a rotation. Every six months, a batch of new graduates would join the team. As soon as the team began to make progress, they'd all leave, and the company would move to the next team. They'd be assisted by interns, who might stick around for three to six months. The team didn't have any real leadership from the business side, which meant that they essentially almost started over twice a year. Not surprisingly, that project still isn't done.

DON'T FORGET SOFT SKILLS

A lot of companies overemphasize hiring hard skills. Sometimes they look for familiarity with a technology or language, sometimes experience in an industry or domain. While these are no doubt important and necessary qualifications, the soft skills of a data scientist—curiosity, humility, collaboration—are just as important as their hard skills.

Soft skills can be harder to define on a paper résumé but are incredibly valuable when working as a team to ship machine learning based software. Because of the wide diversity of skills, experience, and needs an AI team has, the team's data scientists will have to be able to communicate with people who don't understand their hard skills. They'll need to talk about what they'll need from others and what they can offer to the team in order for the team as a whole to be successful.

They'll also need the humility to recognize that their years of school and experience aren't the only things they need to produce software. Hiring a big ego or someone with something to prove will always end badly; it'll be extremely challenging for them to be successful working as part of a team.

That need for soft skills doubles for the team's manager. The most important thing a manager can do is make everyone feel known and heard, creating a safe environment for people to talk and work. When team members have a personal sense of security and trust in the team, they'll communicate and collaborate.

These needs aren't specific to AI teams, of course. Every book on management will tell you the same thing. But AI-based software requires such a diversity of viewpoints, backgrounds, and roles that you'd be remiss not to prioritize an ability to collaborate when choosing who to hire.

No matter the structure and composition of your team, the most important thing your organization must provide is clarity of mission. From the very beginning, the organization has to understand and embrace the problems they're asking the team to solve. They can enable that team to be successful by giving them a clear mission and the support they need to accomplish it. When it's time to move the models to production, they need to have a culture of responsibility and governance, to make sure security and ethical considerations are managed.

Building an AI solution takes the support of the entire organization. It took Figure Eight a while to realize that, but you don't have to wait. Structure your AI teams correctly from the beginning. Only a cross-functional team can handle the multifaceted kind of problem that AI can solve.

We've talked about the basic steps required to set up AI. Next, we'll discuss how to implement AI in detail, from your first Goldilocks pilot problem to a fully scaled-out production process.

CHAPTER 6

CREATING A SUCCESSFUL PILOT

"Never doubt that a small group of thoughtful, committed citizens can change the world. Indeed, it is the only thing that ever has."

—MARGARET MEAD

A national media and automotive dealer conglomerate—relied upon by nearly every person buying or selling cars in the country—once tried to get into the AI game in order to mine more information from the big library of images of the used cars they sold. They figured if they could automatically identify dents, rust, and other kinds of damage, they would be able to find all kinds of uses for the information, from scheduling repairs more efficiently to providing accurate descriptions to customers to handling accident claims.

So they asked an AI team to create a model that could find dents and rust in images of cars. The AI team started building the model, but because they knew this was a complex problem, they also subcontracted with several other machine learning companies at the same time, hoping that at least one of them would do the job quickly and accurately.

Over a year and a few million dollars later, none of the models could achieve better than 60 to 70 percent accuracy. The images didn't have uniform lighting, which led to the shading being inconsistent. The model wasn't able to reliably distinguish between dents, rust stains, or simple shadows.

This failure didn't happen for lack of talented computer vision scientists working on the problem. Computer vision problems are notoriously difficult to solve. They require a huge investment in data labeling and complex models that a lot of companies find hard to justify—unless the business value is similarly huge.

This company's mistake was a common one: they started with an AI problem rather than starting with a business problem. They didn't ask the AI team to focus on a solution for a single business pain point. Instead, they handed them a big, general problem and asked them to get it up and running with a certain quality level, and they'd figure out exactly how to use it later. It's no wonder that the team wasn't able to deliver.

In contrast, Twitter is a good example of a company that started with a specific business program in mind and then scaled up to become far more sophisticated over time by using machine learning to solve myriad business problems. Take, for example, the problem of spam or malicious accounts. Between January and June 2017, Twitter deployed a machine-learning-based approach to target terrorist accounts. This approach ended up removing almost 300,000 accounts in six months. Fast forward a few years: between July and December 2019, there were close to 3 million unique pieces of content removed.[33] The pilot they started in 2017 has since scaled up significantly for a variety of broader use cases to keep the platform in check. As recently as the US presidential election in November 2020, Twitter started to monitor more closely for content that was false or misleading to voters and automatically placed disclaimers on tweets containing such information.[34]

The car company didn't set up their pilot to succeed because the problem was too big and general, the data

---

33 Twitter, "Rules Enforcement", https://transparency.twitter.com/en/reports/rules-enforcement. html#2019-jul-dec.

34 Beykpour, Kayvon and Gadde, Vijaya, "Additional steps we're taking ahead of the 2020 US Election", October 2020, https://blog.twitter.com/en_us/topics/company/2020/2020-election-changes.html.

were poorly curated, and the business value was ambiguous. They eventually had to scrap the project because they couldn't justify the expense. In contrast, Autodesk scaled from a single password-reset use to 60 use cases. You're far more likely to achieve success in a project if you set up the pilot correctly in the first place.

WHAT MAKES A GREAT PILOT?

Running a pilot isn't as simple as launching the model in a few business areas and sitting back to watch what happens. A great pilot is intentionally planned and carefully scaled, like Autodesk's. Parameters are clearly defined: the pilot is limited in time, scale, and scope, and run in a controlled environment. A great pilot can even be one that you realize will never make it to production as part of the pilot process. Not all pilots will launch into production, but a bad pilot won't make that distinction clear. Most importantly, a great pilot can be run without impacting core business functions.

According to industry analyst firm Gartner, failures in the pilot stage like the automotive company's are by no means the exception. In fact, only 20 percent of AI pilots in the real world make it to production. The other 80 percent fail for the reasons we've discussed in previous chapters: not picking the right problem, not having a clear strategy, not having the right team, not creating a sustainable data infrastructure, or neglecting security or ethical considerations. Pilots can fail because their success isn't measurable or because their goals aren't realistic or achievable. Above all, pilots fail when they aren't designed to address a business need directly.

Even though 80 percent of projects currently fail, there's good news. A majority of the problems that these projects encounter are not only solvable, but with the right planning ahead of time, they can be avoided altogether. By working with our clients to ensure they apply these best practices, we've seen a solid 67 percent make it to production.

The following worksheet can be used to help you to articulate your problem's value to your business. It will also encourage collaboration between the business and technical staff.

AREA	QUESTION	YOUR ANSWERS	EXAMPLE
Goal	What is the top-line business goal? Specific Measurable Achievable Realistic Timely (SMART)		We want to increase Annual Recurring Revenue (ARR) from North America-based prospects by 15 percent in the first half of 2021.
	What is the top-line business goal of this pilot? (SMART)		We want to increase Annual Recurring Revenue ARR from California-based prospects by 15 percent in June 2021.
	Why is this goal valuable and important to solve?		This is valuable to our shareholders and would materially increase our stock price and value as a company. It would ensure long-term company stability because California represents our largest addressable market.
	What success criteria will this be evaluated on?		Functional prototype completed and in production based on percentage of goal achieved (0-100 percent).
Team	What stakeholder(s) benefits from achieving this goal the most?		1. VP of Sales, North America 2. _____ 3. _____

AREA	QUESTION	YOUR ANSWERS	EXAMPLE
Strategy	Is this problem well suited for machine learning?		Yes. There is a repetitive task, which has narrow decision criteria that is well understood, and has high human agreement, and there is a significant volume of available relevant data that can be processed for training.
	What is the problem you are solving?		The outbound sales development team doesn't have the tools or time to find the best contacts to reach out to, so it ends up reaching out to many who aren't the ideal customer profile, with low response rates.
	What level of new investment is required?		Five people, eight weeks, and $50,000.
Bias	What bias or ethical considerations are there with this pilot?		Our dataset over-indexes on men as most likely to be purchasers. Is this appropriate or substantiated in the dataset? How should our pilot account for this?

AREA	QUESTION	YOUR ANSWERS	EXAMPLE
Execution	How will this goal be achieved? [Use case short explanation]		We will increase the quality and quantity of prospects we are contacting outbound by automatically sourcing and prioritizing those most likely to respond to and resonate with our messaging.
	What components do you need to build to achieve the goals of this pilot?		1. URL links of profiles targeted in the last three months. 2. Ability to scrape, store, and edit data from those profiles. 3. Trained model.
	Are there off-the-shelf models that are acceptable?		No.
	What data do you need more specifically to train a model?		Name, title, description, employment history (titles, company, company size), date contacted, contact text, response (y/n), response text, response sentiment, date responded, purchased (y/n), purchased date, and purchase amount.
	What (if any) annotation do you need on this data?		Contact text and response sentiment.
	What team is needed to achieve this?		Software engineer, data scientist, project management, and business analyst.

AREA	QUESTION	YOUR ANSWERS	EXAMPLE
Data annotation	What does the sample data to be annotated look like?		Thanks for your email, but I'm not interested at this time.
	How quickly will you need the data?		Two weeks into the pilot kick-off date.
	How much data do you need for this pilot?		At least 25,000 examples of overall LinkedIn profiles and associated data, with at least 5,000 examples of responses and 1,000 examples of purchase behavior.
	What are the instructions to annotate the data?		Does this contact response have a sentiment of wanting to continue chatting or engaging? Positive, negative, too hard to tell.
	What are the quality requirements and evaluation criteria?		Three judgments overlap. 90 percent adherence to gold standard test questions.
	What languages are contained in the dataset?		English.
	What data and technological security considerations are appropriate?		Proprietary, company confidential data should not leave company premises. Secure data handling required.
	What people (crowd) security considerations are appropriate?		NDA required.

Pilots might succeed on their own, but unless you think through how they'll be put into production ahead of time, the project as a whole will fail. How will it be integrated into a business workflow, and who will be needed to do that integration work? The model isn't useful sitting on someone's laptop; it's only going to pay off when it's in a production environment, providing value.

In April 2015, California was experiencing a terrible drought. Governor Jerry Brown issued mandatory water restrictions: municipalities had to cut their water usage by 25 percent within the next few months. This presented an enormous challenge to local governments. They could ask everyone to use less water, but some wouldn't be able to or wouldn't listen. If the city could find people who were using more than their fair share, however, they could reach out directly to help them cut back. Unfortunately, few cities in California had the sophistication or metering to understand exactly where all their water was going.[35]

OmniEarth® was a small California-based startup that analyzed public satellite imagery to provide data about water usage. They looked at the color of lawns—if a lawn was too green, it probably meant that a lot of water went

---

35 Nagourney, Adam, "California Imposes First Mandatory Water Restrictions to Deal With Drought", *The New York Times*, April 2015, https://www.nytimes.com/2015/04/02/us/california-imposes-first-ever-water-restrictions-to-deal-with-drought.html.

into keeping it that way. A house with solar panels on its roof was an indicator the home was statistically more likely to have other green efficiencies inside, like low-flow showers or toilets. Considering these and other factors, OmniEarth was able to provide very granular consumption data to California's water district about how much water every property actually needed.[36]

While OmniEarth's model was very successful at telling if someone's lawn was too green, that didn't help the water districts of California identify who they should get in contact with. The model had to be integrated with actual billing data to show which properties were using more water than they needed. In the first district they integrated, an employee at the water company looked up his own home address to test the system—and was surprised to learn that he was a big offender! It turned out he had a leak in his backyard, but it took a successful model integrated with billing data to identify it as overconsumption of water.

As a result of this integration, California cities were able to target their direct-mail campaigns very narrowly to only those people who were overconsuming water. This efficiency allowed their budgets to stretch a lot further and

---

36 Griggs, Mary Beth, "IBM Watson Can Help Find Water Wasters In Drought-Stricken California", *Popular Science*, May 2016, https://www.popsci.com/how-watson-supercomputer-can-see-water-waste-in-drought-stricken-california/.

ultimately help them be more successful at achieving the aggressive goal the governor had mandated.

OmniEarth didn't start with the entire state of California; they started with a single county and worked their way up. If they'd tried to apply the same model everywhere in California, it wouldn't have worked. The meaning of "too green" is very different in the Sierra Nevada than it is in Los Angeles or the Bay Area. Even though they knew the ultimate goal was the entire state, they scaled down their pilot to a single county, which allowed them to be successful.

But that didn't mean their pilot project could make choices that would prohibit scaling up. For example, since they were working in a single county, they could have acquired far more detailed imagery by sending up drones. This might have made it easier to get their pilot model to succeed, but it clearly wouldn't have been possible for the entire state. Nor could they have used their own images for the pilot but switched to the publicly available US Geological Survey data for the state. The data would be materially different; there's no guarantee the same model would work with both. Instead, they relied on the USGS data from the beginning since they knew ahead of time that they'd be able to replicate their results when the time came to expand. Even with the definition of "too much water" being different from county to county, the data they used would still scale to the whole state. OmniEarth's approach was ultimately considered very successful, and the company was acquired by EagleView® in 2017.[37]

GET PREPARED TO SCALE UP

As we've said, it's important to set up your pilot for success to help build confidence in the solution and prepare your organization for future AI projects. But the purpose of the pilot isn't just to create a successful pilot and stop there. Never lose sight of the long-term goal—everything accomplished in the pilot stage should later be possible in production.

You should design your pilot to be small in scale but with the ability to scale up while keeping the processes and outcomes consistent. Hopefully, all you have to do to scale up is spend more on resources. For every decision you make in the pilot, ask: will I also be able to do this at production scale? Will I be able to integrate this into a production environment just as well? If your pilot takes shortcuts by relying on some unique feature of the smaller scope that would be cost-prohibitive at scale, or needs data that doesn't exist for the entire production scope, or simply isn't technically possible, then your project will fail even if your pilot succeeds.

---

37 Jeff Foust, "OmniEarth Acquired by EagleView, Continuing Satellite-Imagery Consolidation Wave." *SpaceNews*, 28 Apr. 2017, https://spacenews.com/omniearth-acquired-by-eagleview/.

People often assume that once a model is built, it'll scale out in production with only marginal increases in costs. Usually, these people are disappointed. AI solutions aren't like a SaaS business, where resource consumption increases only marginally as new customers are brought on. They have to be supplied with new data continuously in order to work and adapt to inevitable changes in the real world. Depending on the problem you're solving, your model may need to be retrained frequently or need to be fed data for every new customer. It's even possible, although not common, that your AI costs will scale closer to linearly with usage.

Even if you don't have high costs for your pilot, it should still help you predict what your production costs will be. This can let you budget effectively and also maximize the efficiency of your platform spend on AWS or Google or Azure®—if you buy GPUs for a full year, they're much cheaper than allocating them on demand. The pilot process, if correctly structured, will let you capitalize on those savings.

In the end, if done right, the costs should be worth it. Think about it; without the AI model, you'd have to scale all your business operations manually to do the same things you're automating. Even with that extra investment, it'll be cheaper and will get you better results. It'll also help surface security and ethical problems before they become serious—something that, as we've discussed, you should be hypervigilant in watching out for. The decisions you make in the pilot stage could easily have ethical implications in production.

BACK TO BUSINESS OBJECTIVES

It's critical that everyone participating in a machine learning based project really understands the business context. If you're a line-of-business person, your role in creating the pilot will be to reinforce that context as the problem is explored. You've got to keep the team focused on the use case they're trying to solve and help them take the most efficient route to get there.

Don't be afraid to get out of your comfort zone and into the details of the data. In fact, it's downright critical that you get into the details. Business people often assume that data science is too difficult for them to get into directly, but in reality, it's made up of very simple concepts that any average businessperson can wrap their head around. Dive in because it's unlikely that the data science team will be successful without you bridging the gap between the model and the business. Remember Alyssa's experience with the dataset that was accidentally tagged in a way that had terribly offensive consequences in output? The data science team couldn't solve the problem alone; it took a businessperson to engage with the bigger picture.

There's a lot to consider, but hopefully, you've learned that it's completely possible to set up a successful pilot. It's never going to be easy. The odds are against you. But you can be successful if you follow this structure.

Of course, once your pilot is successful, you'll actually have to take it into production and make it successful in the long-term. In the next chapter, we'll help you learn to adapt to the problems you may encounter on that journey.

CHAPTER 7

THE JOURNEY TO PRODUCTION

"It is not enough to give money for demonstration projects. From the very beginning, plans should be made for the scaling-up of successful innovations."

—RUTH SIMMONS

Alyssa

The early team that I worked with on the visual recognition product at Watson was very small and fairly junior. Our first demo, which was mostly built by an intern, was a simple website. You could drag-and-drop any image you had lying around on your desktop or phone, press a button, and be presented with a list of tags describing what was in the image. For example, this image of my sister and me at a wedding would come back with tags such as "woman" and "bridesmaids." Simple enough.

The website itself wasn't the product, of course; the API underneath it was. We had built the website demo as a play toy that people who weren't comfortable using the API directly, like businesspeople, could use to understand what the system could do. It wasn't meant to be used broadly, so we hadn't put any dedicated QA resources on it. A few team members and I had gone through it to make sure it was mostly working, and we'd found a few bugs, which had been fixed. It was a little fragile but good enough for the scale we were expecting. This was essentially an internal sales tool for us to use and demo to customers one at a time.

We launched the demo on a Wednesday and sent the link to a few interested salespeople. We expected no more than a hundred people to be accessing the system at a given time; honestly, I thought we would be lucky if a dozen folks used it at once. In reality, I could barely get my mother to open the link. I was hoping that as many as a thousand people would access the demo in the first month.

I left for a business trip to Boston on Thursday. I was supposed to be in New York on Monday, so I was staying with a friend of mine for the weekend when my phone started blowing up on Saturday morning. After a few angry calls, I finally figured out what had happened. Somehow, our little demo had been put on Reddit, and by Saturday morning, it was on the front page.

Suddenly, our webpage, built by an intern, was receiving thousands of visitors every minute, instead of the few we'd imagined. We hadn't set it up for scale, so the system attempted to automatically scale up to handle the extra traffic—and didn't handle it particularly well. This somehow exposed some underlying bugs in the supporting system architecture the demo was built on top of, which ended up bringing down an entire IBM data center in the southern US for about 20 minutes. Fortunately, IBM has lots and lots of backup procedures in place, so we didn't end up doing any actual damage to anyone, but there were more than a few hours where I was terrified of the harm I may have caused unintentionally.

The actual machine learning product, the API built on Watson, was just fine; it was the demo toy website we'd written that couldn't handle the load. But to the outside world, it looked as if Watson itself wasn't working. The Reddit comments said things like: "We brought down Watson."[38] As a product manager, this was a scary moment. This was potentially significant bad press for IBM—way above my pay grade. As you can imagine, my general manager learned who I was that day, and it was not a good thing. She was not pleased with the team or me for being so careless with a demo launch.

I was beside myself, trying to get to a computer so that I could get on Slack and notify the right people to deal with the problem. Luckily, everything was fixed in less than an hour, and no one's business suffered any major impact. But I learned a big lesson about putting systems in production without anticipating what might happen.

No matter how hard you try to keep your pilot consistent with your expectations for the production system, it will always be different. Sometimes you can predict what will be different, and sometimes you can't. But developing an appreciation for the fact that production and the pilot

---

38 "r/InternetIsBeautiful - Give IBM's Watson an Image, and It Will Try to Guess What's in It." *Reddit*, www.reddit.com/r/InternetIsBeautiful/comments/4azkue/give_ibms_watson_an_image_and_it_will_try_to/.

will be different will help you prepare for it. Plan to pivot as you go.

If the machine learning product you're working on is valuable and interesting, which you'd hope it would be, it has the potential to reach a scale that is much larger than more mundane applications. Machine learning applications often enable something cool or interesting that couldn't be done before. When they make it into the real world, people often try to use them in ways you didn't expect.

At a minimum, the scale in production will be greater, and the data different; both of these will materially change your outcomes in unanticipated ways. While a pilot typically deals with a narrow use case, a production deployment may broaden the use case slightly, along with the volume. No matter how much testing you do on the pilot, it may not expose edge cases that you'll discover at scale. Every stage of the process has some risk. But if you plan for that risk, you'll be in a much better position than if you didn't.

PLAN AHEAD

Before you're even close to putting your model into production, you should try to get clarity on what your production pain points will be. These can affect the framework, libraries, or language you'll use in production; how and where you'll deploy your model; and the ways you'll need to monitor it.

One major e-commerce company embarked on an NLP project to perform sentiment analysis on their chatbot logs. Their goal was to follow up personally with customers that had a negative experience. To get started, they prototyped everything in Python (a programming language commonly used by data scientists), which has a host of NLP libraries available. But when it came time to deploy the model to production, they discovered they'd have to port the entire model to Scala (a programming language used by software engineers to build highly scalable software) so that it could run in the Java environment they had available.

Will you need to scale your training or scale your inference? It can be trivially simple to train the model on a single machine and distribute requests to the inference model, but it's much harder to do distributed training. Many of the common training algorithms run on a single node, updating the entire model at once for each data point. Luckily, some libraries, like TensorFlow, can help spread that training out across a cluster of machines— another reason it's important to analyze your production needs well in advance.

The following are three important areas you need to consider when planning to deploy your model to production:

- Availability: Make sure there are no interruptions in service, even during upgrades or deploys. If your AI model is used in a business-critical application or an end-user facing product, a system outage can cost a lot of money. On August 19, 2013, Amazon was down for 30 minutes, which theoretically cost it $66,240 per minute, or nearly $2 million. That number would be much higher today.[39]

- Performance: Make sure it responds quickly enough. For the majority of production systems, the faster the site speed, the higher the user-conversion rate. Walmart found that for every one-second improvement in page-load times, conversions increased by two percent.[40] COOK increased conversions by seven percent by reducing page-load time by 0.85 seconds.[41] No one wants to use a slow product anyway. So make sure your AI model is performing well and doesn't slow down your product.

- Scalability: How much traffic can it handle now? How does it handle an increase in demand—scale out, scale up? You need to consider how many users will use your

39   Clay, Kelly. "Amazon.com Goes Down, Loses $66,240 Per Minute." *Forbes*, Forbes Magazine, 19 Aug. 2013, https://www.forbes.com/sites/kellyclay/2013/08/19/amazon-com-goes-down-loses-66240-per-minute/#5d01ccee495c.

40   Green, Viki, "Impact of slow page load time on website performance", January 2016, https://medium.com/@vikigreen/impact-of-slow-page-load-time-on-website-performance-40d5c9ce568a.

41   Winkler, Nick, "Performance vs. Functionality: Making the Right Site Speed Tradeoffs", *ShopifyPlus*, August 2020, https://www.shopify.com/enterprise/performance-vs-functionality-making-the-right-site-speed-tradeoffs.

product, which is supported by your AI model. More importantly, if the user base increases in the future, consider how your AI model will continue to support that increase.

When people build prototypes or do research, they may try complicated AI models and use expensive hardware. However, you have to consider the cost of the computational power in production and if your AI model is too complicated to support the availability, performance, and scalability needed by the business. The rule of thumb here is that if a simple model can do the job, don't pick the complicated one if their performance is on par.

ADAPT TO CHANGE

Another common issue that might crop up at scale is gaps or holes in your data that you didn't consider during the pilot. If this happens, you'll have to adapt, either by finding data to fill the holes or narrowing the scope of the model, so there are no holes.

The US Department of Defense Joint Artificial Intelligence Agency uses AI detection technology to help first responders deal with emergencies. During the California wildfires in 2018, they were critical in helping firefighters deal with the 8,500 fires across 1.9 million acres. One of the challenges they ran into, however, was that, because fires are impossible to predict in advance, the aerial images of fires don't have a direct bearing on future fires. A pilot model trained on historical data has to be materially different from one that can be used in production because the data needed to train a model to predict a fire simply doesn't exist. In this situation, however, the lack of training data could be managed by reducing the expectations of the model. Even a lower-accuracy prediction can assist in damage control and save lives and property by comparing current fire trends to historical ones. This allows the fire departments to route teams and equipment more efficiently. While not every home can be saved by these predictions, they help to reduce fire damage and make firefighting more efficient. AI has been used similarly in California during the 2019 and 2020 wildfire seasons.[42]

Machine learning models, of course, are designed to process input. But you may find that once you release a solution into the wild, people will give it input you didn't anticipate. In some cases, this can be a security problem. Take, for example, Siri or Alexa, which were designed to answer people's general knowledge questions and perform some simple actions—turn on the lights, play a podcast, describe the weather. They were not, however, designed to handle secure, sensitive information. If someone asks Siri

42   McCormick, John. "California Firefighters Tap AI for an Edge in Battling Wildfires." *The Wall Street Journal*, Dow Jones & Company, 1 Oct. 2020, https://www.wsj.com/articles/california-firefighters-tap-ai-for-an-edge-in-battling-wildfires-11601544600.

or Alexa to remember their credit card or social security numbers, they will. It's unlikely the initial model designers anticipated the need to protect that kind of sensitive data.

One way to handle this might be to include a legal disclaimer saying that the system isn't designed for personal information. Another might be to create more security around data in general. In either case, you can tailor your response to the specific problem that arises. What's important is that you adapt when necessary.

Compliance issues often raise their heads in production. In some cases, laws can change out from under your model. The usage rights you have to your data might change. Even if compliance risks during the pilot stage are low, it's worth going through the plan with lawyers well before you go into production. They could easily uncover something that might have scrapped your whole project, giving you a chance to deal with it. Where did you get your training data? Do you have the rights to use it for this purpose? If your model makes a decision that has liability implications—for example, providing analysis that leads to the denial of an insurance claim—can you explain how it made the decision in a way that will pass legal muster?

Ensuring that your system can adapt to novel information and a changing reality is key to making sure that it's sustainable and has a shelf life longer than the time it took to train it. The world moves fast; what was true two weeks ago may no longer be so. Any news cycle could drastically change consumer or purchasing behaviors and render your usage of your model ineffective or useless.

It's naive to think that you do it once and you're done. Machine learning technology inherently changes over time as the data training it changes; you have to be able to adapt to deal with it. Adaptability is key for a sustainable, long-term business. Your business needs to incorporate new ideas or different customer behaviors as they evolve, which naturally should be reflected and translated into your machine learning models as well.

SECURITY

If your system is available in any kind of public way, you'll have to guard against bad actors. People with malicious intent will try all sorts of things in order to defeat your model.

Spammers have come up with all kinds of clever ways to trick machine learning models designed to filter them out into letting their emails through. One of the most popular techniques is adversarial input. They'll constantly try changing the format or content of their messages until they find some loophole the model doesn't detect. They can then use that to evade filtering until the model can be retrained.

You can protect against adversarial input first by limiting the amount of probing that bad actors can do—for example, by rate-limiting requests from the same IP or account or requiring the user to solve a CAPTCHA if they make frequent requests. In certain cases, it's appropriate to keep the details of your model secret, so attackers won't have any hints as to where they can probe.

Some very sophisticated attackers might even try to recreate your model by training their own version with the results from yours. In some cases, they can even analyze these results to discover details of your training data, which might contain sensitive information. There are many techniques to deal with this problem and keep your models private, but, like with adversarial input, you'll also be able to reduce an attacker's ability to steal your model by limiting their access.

If your AI application responds to feedback—for example, a chatbot that learns from conversation or a rating system—you can assume that malicious users will try to skew it to behave badly. Remember Tay, Microsoft's chatbot that 4chan turned into a racist in less than a day? 4chan also got CNN's mobile app removed from the App Store and Google Play Store by coordinating a flood of artificial one-star reviews.[43]

---

43   Willens, Max, "CNN's mobile app is under siege from Trump supporters", *Digiday*, July 2017, https://digiday.com/media/cnns-mobile-app-siege-trump-supporters/.

In both cases, the damage could have been mitigated by delaying the effect of the feedback until it could be confirmed as valid. If Tay had waited to apply what it learned until a human had looked over the conversations it was having, or if Apple or Google had investigated a sudden increase in one-star ratings before blacklisting an app, these problems could have been avoided. Instead, feedback was directly applied, and public actions were taken without the authenticity of the incoming data ever being assessed. Even if you do a perfect job, you're likely to encounter attacks you couldn't possibly predict. That's why it's vital to set up a process to recover from incidents when attacks happen. The operations team will need to know who they should call. You'll need to document how to shut down your model while you solve the problem or how to roll it back to some alternate version that might not be susceptible to the current attack.

Before I put our visual recognition demo into production, I should have made sure we had a monitoring system in place to alert us to as many different scenarios as we could think of, or at least give us visibility when things went wrong. As it was, I only knew there was a problem when I started getting angry phone calls. Rookie mistake. No excuse for that blunder.

I also should have had more robust scale testing. Even though I didn't expect more than a few hundred people to look at the demo, it was publicly available, and it was cool (kudos to the team!). In 2015, it was novel to be able to tag a picture from your own computer using machine learning. This wasn't the kind of thing that your average consumer interacted with. I should have anticipated that it was at least possible for it to get a lot more attention than I predicted.

For some use cases, it's important to consider internal security as well. Boeing® and other companies who make planes have been early adopters of robotic automation and machine learning. There are layers upon layers of machine learning based systems that essentially automatically fly most commercial flights between points A and B, depending on the regulations for different airspaces around the world.[44] Consider what havoc a bad actor inside a company who has access to training or controlling these systems could do! It's critical to have tightly regulated governance over who has access to these systems. Certainly, not every use case is self-flying planes—but every production deployment should consider the potential for security implications.

---

44 Stewart, Jack. "Don't Freak Over Boeing's Self-Flying Plane—Robots Already
    Run the Skies." *Wired*, Conde Nast, 12 June 2017, https://www.wired.com/story/
    boeing-autonomous-plane-autopilot/.

| CHAPTER 8 |

LEADING WITH AI

"As leaders, it is incumbent on all of us to make sure we are building a world in which every individual has an opportunity to thrive. Understanding what AI can do and how it fits into your strategy is the beginning, not the end, of that process."

—ANDREW NG, CO-FOUNDER OF GOOGLE BRAIN

Leading with AI doesn't just happen in the blink of an eye. Amazon, a leader in machine learning technology applications, didn't start out using advanced AI techniques on day one. Just like everyone else, they had to go on a journey filled with discovery, successes—and the occasional course correction. For example, in 2017, Amazon launched a TV ad that accidentally triggered Alexa devices in its customers' homes to purchase an expensive dollhouse.[45] Not

---

45   Liptak, Andrew, "Amazon's Alexa started ordering people dollhouses after hearing its name on TV", *The Verge*, January 2017, https://www.theverge.com/2017/1/7/14200210/amazon-alexa-tech-news-anchor-order-dollhouse.

ideal, and not the best advertisement for the convenience of their machine learning devices.

They stuck with progress, though, and learned from their mistakes. Their greatest asset has been their dogged focus on generating business value in diverse, myriad ways across the entire company. As they've developed their machine learning technology, they've gotten especially good at a few important things:

They recognized that their executive leadership needed to embed AI throughout the company to help a huge variety of teams with everyday business problems.

They created cross-functional teams to optimize AI support functions like data annotation, management, governance, and deployment.

They were persistent, even though they started out behind the pack. Their focus on incremental progress meant that it only took five short years for Alexa to beat out Siri and Google Assistant in the smart home speaker market.[46] Alexa may have had a slow start, but now she's a very strong player in the market.

Persistence and determination are the ingredients that build leaders in AI—not perfection from the start.

---

46   Kinsella, Bret, "Amazon Alexa Has 82 Percent Smart Speaker Market Share", *Voicebot.ai*, June 2017, https://voicebot.ai/2017/06/23/amazon-alexa-82-percent-smart-speaker-market-share/.

Another example of persistence in AI comes from The New York Times. The past decade saw a landmark shift in the way news is delivered and consumed by the US public. Print media, already on a decline throughout the first decade of the century, took a nosedive. Since 2010, more than 2,000 US newspapers—from local papers to major metro dailies—either drastically reduced print publication and coverage or shuttered operations completely.

Yet The New York Times, along with a small handful of publications, didn't just survive the so-called "death of print media"—the newspaper of record thrived within the new paradigm, skillfully shifting the bulk of its footprint from the printed page to the internet. As of August 2020, The New York Times boasts 6.5 million subscribers.[47]

What made the difference?

There isn't just one answer; an array of competitive advantages added up to The New York Times' dominance in media over the past decade. One such advantage: The New York Times was an early adopter of AI integration in business systems. The organization prioritized AI adoption across a variety of use cases.

Moving from print to online engagement with readership

47   Tracy, Marc. "Digital Revenue Exceeds Print for 1st Time for New York Times Company." *The New York Times*, The New York Times, 5 Aug. 2020, www.nytimes.com/2020/08/05/business/media/nyt-earnings-q2.html.

is a challenging transition for any publication. After all, the immediacy and relative anonymity of the internet creates a rich new environment for dialogue; anyone with an internet connection is invited to comment on any article. However, many other publications switching to an internet model in the 2010s struggled to balance open accessibility with the need to maintain reputability. As anyone who's spent time on YouTube can attest, comment sections, when left unchecked, can quickly turn into a display that robs a source of its gravitas. The New York Times faced the same problem as everyone else: how do you keep readers engaged, active, and vocal, without spending an arm and a leg to moderate the resulting minefield of comments?

Moderating comments by hand wasn't a scalable solution for an institution like The New York Times, which doesn't provide that kind of forum as its core business. Rather than abandoning an important channel for receiving valuable feedback and inquiries, however, they turned to AI to solve the problem. They chose to use Perspective API, a sophisticated machine learning based content moderation product developed by Jigsaw® (an Alphabet subsidiary) to detect and filter scams and abusive comments.[48] As a result, they were able to take full advantage of the direct interaction the internet allows without compromising their reputation as a trusted institution.

48   Adams, CJ. "New York Times: Using AI to Host Better Conversations." *Google*, Google, 23 May 2018, blog.google/technology/ai/new-york-times-using-ai-host-better-conversations/.

This is just one example of how The New York Times has embedded AI into their business. Put simply, they're not just a print company anymore. They're not an AI company, either. They're a media company that has woven AI-based solutions into several pockets of their operations. They— along with many companies in the same boat—have managed to rise to the challenge of an industry undergoing rapid disruption by harnessing the fundamental, transformational force of AI.

This didn't happen overnight.

World-class AI takes a lot of effort, a large investment over time, and a huge mindset shift throughout the company culture. A company can't simply set up a small innovation team to solve point problems. The entire organization must invest in identifying opportunities for taking advantage of the technology and incorporating it into every team's operations, restructuring the company's metrics and goals, reorganizing teams, and hiring new people to tackle these challenges.

A company can't just use AI. To gain the advantage, a company must lead with AI.

What does this look like?

Depending on the scale and sophistication of the organization, the specifics will vary widely, but consistently, companies who do this well focus on building these skills holistically across the entire workforce. The organization has to develop muscles it probably doesn't have yet.

IDENTIFYING THE RIGHT PROBLEMS

Before a business can lead with AI, it has to identify problems AI can solve. Finding the Goldilocks problem provides the foundation of what to look for; the next step is putting that concept into consistent action.

You can't accomplish this by building an AI tiger team and turning them loose to hunt through each department for inefficiencies. That AI team wouldn't have the necessary context, and all its time would be spent coming up to speed on the operations of the various departments.

Each division or department is familiar with its own operations and has the context to identify the most important problems. What they might lack is an understanding of AI and the types of problems it can solve. Giving them that training is the first step.

Organizations that do this successfully start with the belief that every department can use AI to solve some of its problems and work toward enabling their leaders to identify and solve those use cases. For example, a CFO, who is presumably good at what they do, probably doesn't have any experience in AI—their expertise lies in finance. That CFO will need training to develop an AI-aware mindset, a capability of identifying the places within the finance department where AI can solve problems. In some cases, this might mean hiring new leaders or someone to assist the existing leader with this skill.

It's tempting to try to avoid the big overhaul by only targeting this training to where you think it's most needed. Maybe one department has more perceived inefficiencies than the others, and you think that if you just bring them up to speed, they'll be able to fix them and start helping other departments find problems in the bargain. Don't fall into this trap; in the long run, this approach is much less efficient.

Every department's AI use cases will be as different as the departments are themselves, so every leader has to be trained to identify problems in their own department. If you teach AI principles to a subset of your department leaders, you'll end up with AI rolling out only in that same subset of your departments. It's much better to teach the entire organization and ingrain this practice into your company's culture.

MANAGING THE DATA PIPELINE

Once the organizations within your business have found

some problems that AI can solve, they're going to need access to data. Your business already produces swaths of data in the normal course of business, but if it's like most companies, that data is stuck in silos, scattered in single-purpose databases. You'll have to develop a more mature, sophisticated approach to managing all that data.

It's extremely common for business data to have all kinds of idiosyncrasies, which the people who use it know how to get around and massage in order to build a report or run a calculation. This simply won't work in an AI world. In order to be used to feed AI models, data needs to be cleaned up, annotated, and prepared.

If the sales organization needs to use some marketing data to feed a model, they can't afford for it to be a custom job every time. The entire company has to become good at organizing and keeping track of its datasets. These datasets have to be made accessible throughout the organization, moved around to train models, and refreshed as new data comes in.

What does building this muscle look like?

More mature and complex organizations will have teams of people dedicated to building data pipelines that can ingest data from different datasets, transform it for general use, and deliver it to the production models that need to use it. Even without dedicated teams, however, your company will have to develop good data hygiene habits from the top down. Just like building the skill to identify AI use cases, this is a cultural shift that has to happen throughout the entire company.

DATA GOVERNANCE

Once problems are identified, data are prepped, and models are rolled out, you'll be faced with a very important question: how can you be sure that the models being rolled out are solving problems in a way that matches the business's priorities?

The answer to that question is data governance. You'll need to institute guidelines and policies that ensure that the data that feed your models are of high quality and the models continue to support the objectives and ethics of the business.

All AI models, at their core, are designed to optimize for some set of metrics. As models are improved, they're tested against the old models. Often, those tests arrive at competing optimizations, where models could improve the performance of one metric at the expense of another. Somebody has to choose which model should go into production. It can't just be the data scientist or department head responsible for that model. They may not have the context to make that decision for the whole business.

Any sophisticated content moderation model, including the one put in place by The New York Times to detect harassing comments, balances the optimization of hundreds of different metrics. Without a clear and transparent governance structure, how can the company decide when one of those metrics should take priority over another?

These decisions can be nuanced and need to synthesize priorities from every department. Should the model be optimized for the removal of inflammatory language or ad revenue? Should it attempt to reduce false positives, which filter out some legitimate comments? Or should it reduce false negatives, which might allow a scam comment through here or there?

Business performance isn't the only metric to take into account. Governance policies should also ensure that models and data are used ethically and responsibly. It's all too easy to optimize the performance of some desired metric and unintentionally create, for example, gender or racial bias in the model, as was the case when the Apple Card created gender bias in its model by focusing on other metrics and excluding gender as an input. Every new model has to be evaluated with all these competing priorities in mind.

On top of all these considerations is the problem of security. The company has to make sure that the people moving, transforming, and joining all this data have the right to view it and build on it. Some datasets may be sensitive, containing personal information. Even if the information is publicly available, it may not be appropriate or necessary to use it for your model.

When the use of sensitive datasets is appropriate, how should the company communicate that it's being used? Facebook, for example, has a clear right in its terms of service to use any photos uploaded to its service for any purpose, but that doesn't mean they should.[49]

Luckily, the concept of data governance is far from new. It's been considered in depth by many companies and organizations, and you can jump-start your company's own governance with what they've learned. The World Economic Forum® has produced excellent templates and guidelines, as has the Allen Institute for AI. Other companies that have dealt with this need have presented their results at conferences or in articles. You can adopt these outright or, more likely, use them to come up with one that makes sense for your business.

CROSS-FUNCTIONAL COMPANY

In Chapter 7, we discussed the need to assemble a multi-disciplinary team to deploy an AI pilot project successfully.

---

49   Facebook, "Terms of Service", https://www.facebook.com/terms.php.

When AI is scaled out to the entire company, the same principle applies. The organization as a whole must become highly effective at multidisciplinary communication and collaboration.

At its simplest, this might involve rolling out something like Slack to improve communication across departments. Some companies might adopt Agile processes and workflows to encourage collaborative planning of requirements and provide a mechanism for departments to adapt to changes originating from the outside, as Figure Eight did. The company might institute regular all-hands meetings to sync up business priorities all at once and provide transparency.

The details will be different for every organization, but every company will have a need for departments to collaborate more than before to identify common problems, prepare and share data, and develop related models. In some cases, this may be best served by restructuring the organization and reporting lines; in others, a department that expects an extensive adoption of AI—marketing, for example—may need to establish its own data science team.

This degree of change may seem overwhelming. A big skill gap needs to be filled, and the changes necessary to fill it may seem drastic. It's important, however, for organizations to avoid the short-term solution of creating an AI team that's shared across the company, acting as a vendor to other departments, or that team will end up being the primary bottleneck blocking AI adoption.

BUDGET AND RESOURCE ALLOCATION

Finding the budget to implement AI solutions—to buy off-the-shelf products, hire people with the needed skills, spend time and resources annotating data—is also a common blocker for companies looking to scale their AI. Since a good portion of the investment has to be made company-wide up front, it can take reallocation of significant money and people, both of which are, in most cases, already budgeted out to normal operations. Deciding how much to reallocate and from where will impact the entire organization. But the company needs to understand the promise of the long-term gains that led to this investment. Cutting costs is always unpopular, but if the company can develop an attitude of leading with AI with an understanding of the ultimate payoff, it will have a far greater likelihood of success.

Take, for example, a company eager to invest in AI that runs a call center to capture support calls, return requests, and complaints. There's no magical pool of money sitting around to invest in AI to improve this call center. Instead, the company will have to take money out of the yearly budget to spend on the AI initiative and just accept that the time to handle a call will go up for a period because fewer agents are deployed to receive those calls. The promise, of course, is that the investment in AI will lead to a chatbot that can divert 15 percent of those incoming calls, requiring fewer agents to handle calls and improving the call-handling time overall. This is the type of business focus that will help increase investment in AI. With a clearly articulated cost savings goal, the project will have a clear metric for success.

BUILDING THE MUSCLES

Each of these major muscles will need to be developed by the organization in order to scale AI. Although they're all equally important, they won't all need to be built simultaneously. The first step will be to train large volumes of people to identify AI use cases. As that skill grows within the organization and use cases begin to be identified, the need for the others will rise in priority naturally.

Some companies will be able to leapfrog the muscle-building process via acquisition. When Appen decided they wanted to incorporate technology as a larger component of their business and lead with AI, they hired a CTO and a small team and began the process of developing these muscles.

A few months later, however, they encountered an opportunity to acquire a company that already had many of the skills, people, and technologies that could shortcut some of this lengthy process. The initial team that had been hired to start down the AI path the long way changed focus to weaving this ready-made technology team into the existing business that needed to take advantage of it.

While this option won't be available to every organization starting down this path, this does show progress can be accelerated by thinking about the problem creatively and taking advantage of opportunities. There's no one-size-fits-all approach. Every company will be different and can accomplish this in its own way.

This process is hard. It will take time and massive invest-ment. It's never easy to switch up the operation of huge chunks of a business, reorganize reporting structures, and refocus priorities; it will almost certainly require killing some sacred cows. Even with the long-time horizon and disruption of the familiar, however, it can be done well and is worth it.

Amazon and The New York Times, for example, took years to make this transition. Now, on the other side, they've maintained their status as leaders in their industries, with the infrastructure and culture that enables them to implement new AI solutions throughout their businesses as opportunities and problems arise.

As you begin rolling out changes and developing these skills, keep track of your progress to see how far you've come. Track the number of models that you have in production, how frequently those models are used, and how frequently those models are updated. Taken together, these give a rough idea of your progress.

If a model in production is used hundreds of times per second but is never updated, there's a good deal of risk involved; the data governance surrounding that model and its data sources may need some maturing. In The New York Times example, if they had deployed their content moderation system, but no one ever wrote any comments, the model wouldn't be used very much, and therefore probably wouldn't be that important. The absolute number of models will vary by company and by use case, but if the number of actively used, maintained, and matured models goes up, you're probably on the right track.

Even when models have been created and are used and maintained, the task isn't over. The business, its customers and products, and the data it produces will certainly change. You cannot build world-class AI without a coherent data strategy that allows your AI to adapt over time.

CHAPTER 9

REACHING AI MATURITY

"In a growth mindset, challenges are exciting rather than threatening. So rather than thinking, oh, I'm going to reveal my weaknesses, you say, wow, here's a chance to grow."

—CAROL S. DWECK

In 2017, Google found itself under fire. Parents had discovered that the YouTube Kids filter, whose purpose is to block inappropriate content for children, was failing to identify and block videos that included popular children's characters in sexual situations.[50] Companies had pulled their ads once they'd learned their ads had been shown

---

50 "On YouTube Kids, Startling Images Slip Past Filters", *The New York Times*, November 2017, https://www.nytimes.com/2017/11/04/business/media/youtube-kids-paw-patrol.html.

on YouTube alongside videos that contained exploitative comments about children, hate speech, and extremism.

To deal with the problem, the company hired thousands of content moderators, expanding their video review workforce to over 10,000 employees. Even with this massive assembly, machine learning was also needed to make faster progress. YouTube used machine learning to identify as much problematic content as possible, then employed human reviewers not only to remove content directly but also to identify training data that could be used to improve the machine learning applications.[51]

Google's machine learning models improved the speed, accuracy, and scale of human moderation by 5x. By Q2 of 2018, 10 million videos had been removed by moderators; 75 percent of those videos were removed without a single view. Today, 98 percent of the extremist videos flagged for removal are flagged by algorithms, and 70 percent of extremist content is removed within eight hours of its upload.

It's hard to draw clear lines between explicit and non-explicit content from a business perspective. This is in part due to the nature of content changes. Standards have to be constantly reviewed, monitored, and updated. In

---

51   Watercutter, Angela, "The Challenge of Making YouTube a Better Place", *Wired*, October 2018, https://www.wired.com/story/wired-25-susan-wojcicki-youtube-moderation/.

addition, models aren't perfect; YouTube needed to have a plan in place to handle the percentage of explicit content that didn't pass the confidence threshold for its model. Because of the scale of the problem at YouTube, that meant employing 10,000 people to review content manually on a daily basis, even after working on the problem for over ten years.

If you're not careful to build a coherent and complete data strategy up front, things can go very wrong, and that valuable data won't end up paying off in the way you'd like. There are five main areas for concern that you can proactively prepare for to ensure your data is handled correctly: quality, completeness, security, governance, and drift.

QUALITY

Alyssa

Years ago, I worked with a global fashion retailer on data annotation in order to support a business goal of a better shopping experience. The specific goal was to provide products relevant to a selected category—for example, when a consumer went to the website and selected "blazer," they wanted to show you a bunch of blazers to choose from. In order to accomplish that, they created training data by taking lots of pictures of their inventory and annotating them by hand, deciding whether or not each picture was of something that could be considered a blazer.

As I looked through the data, I noticed that there was a lot of ambiguity in the association of some pictures with the "blazer" tag. I'm not an expert in fashion, but I think I understand the general concept of what constitutes a blazer. Some of the images that had been given the tag, however, were of what I would consider to be trench coats. One was a blazer made of sweater material that, personally, I would have tagged as a sweater. Where should the line be drawn? This was something the retailer needed to be clear on and able to write down and give examples to back up. What, exactly, made a garment get tagged as a blazer?

It's important to set out specific guidelines about how to tag a piece of data one way or the other. Even in what you would assume would be a simple dataset, like pictures of blazers, there can be nuance. If your annotations are too ambiguous or applied inconsistently, your model won't achieve the intended business outcome.

Without good oversight of the annotation process to ensure narrow, relevant, specific training data, your results will suffer. When a customer searches for blazers, your model might return all kinds of non-blazer tops because you've trained it to believe that nearly anything could be considered a blazer. Your customer experience will be poor, your conversion rate will drop, and your project will have failed.

That doesn't mean that your data shouldn't contain any

ambiguity. Some flexibility in annotation can often produce a better result. Just because my immediate impression of a sweater blazer was that it was a sweater, rather than a blazer, doesn't mean most customers would think the same thing. Someone searching for "blazer" might certainly be looking for something just like it.

During another project with a large voice-assistant company, we were working on categorizing the intent of simple statements. Given the phrase, "What's the weather today?" we would categorize it as having an intent in the category of "weather." There was a matrix of some 50 categories—math, music, business, beauty, etc.

One of the examples that came up was the phrase, "Where is Sally's Beauty Shop?" Immediately, I thought, That's definitely in the "business" category. This person is looking for a business. Someone else on the team, however, insisted that the appropriate category was "beauty." That didn't make any sense to me; if a person interacting with this assistant asked for Sally's Beauty Shop and was given beauty tips and recommendations, they'd be frustrated and have a poor experience with the system. It occurred to me at that moment that I was the only technical woman in the room, and my voice was critical in helping this team build a system that didn't have stark gender bias encoded into it.

A best practice would be to allow the phrase to be categorized in both ways. Neither opinion was necessarily wrong, but choosing one over the other would potentially encode human bias into the system. This is why it is important to not rely on small, insular groups for data labeling and annotation. Quality data annotation comes from large and diverse groups of people because that diversity helps prevent bias and uncover edge cases.

Flexibility in the annotation process is also crucial. With a flexible annotation process, corner cases or ambiguities can be surfaced and addressed at a business level. However, your guidelines need to be flexible but not so flexible that your annotations lose meaning. Make sure the people generating the annotations have some variety of opinion to represent the nuance necessary for your model. At the same time, provide them with an awareness of how the data will be used so they can annotate with intention toward the desired business outcome.

Data quality issues can often arise when business folks don't adequately articulate what "high quality" actually means for a specific use case. Right at the beginning of your project, start by developing a deep understanding of your application's objective and use case. From there, work backward to define the specific criteria necessary for data to be considered of high quality in that context.

This may mean documenting a hundred or a thousand

specific use cases you personally vet that capture all the business purposes the application is meant to support. You'll have to go through all the examples, one by one, and have the business sign off on the appropriate decision to make in each case. It may seem nitty-gritty and tedious, but let me assure you, it is an absolutely critical and valuable use of your time.

The first set of requirements will probably be set by the product manager, but ultimately the process should involve a broad set of stakeholders. The product manager's initial decisions should be vetted by a cross-functional group, including the data scientist, the designer, and other business stakeholders or executives.

In the end, you'll have a document describing what you're going to build, what you plan to control for, and what you don't plan to control for. Depending on the problem, it could be as brief as a few sentences describing some basic decisions, though most real-world problems will probably require significantly more detail.

These decisions may be more or less detailed, depending on the use case. Computer vision recognition decisions have to be very clear and detailed where a home security system is identifying a potential intruder, but can perhaps be more lax if the application is merely identifying social media images that have people in them.

Once you've documented these decisions, they will need to be applied at scale by however many people are responsible for building your application. Because even the most detailed instructions can be misunderstood, you'll also find it highly beneficial to train your annotators. Before beginning on the real dataset, have them practice on a specific use case that highlights some of the potential ambiguities they'll encounter. Provide them with the business context they'll need to interpret the documented decisions.

COMPLETENESS

In 2018, a Tesla Model 3 on autopilot drove into a semi-trailer that had been wedged perpendicular to the freeway, shearing off the roof and killing the driver.[52] Analysis showed the Tesla autopilot system hadn't braked or warned the driver prior to the crash. Why not?

The answer was simple: the autopilot wasn't taught to recognize a truck parked perpendicular to the stream of traffic on the freeway because that scenario happened so infrequently that the dataset the autopilot was trained on wasn't rich and diverse or complete enough to cover this scenario successfully. It's a situation so unusual that

---

52   Lee, Timothy B., "Autopilot was active when a Tesla crashed into a truck, killing driver", *Ars Technica*, May 2019, https://arstechnica.com/cars/2019/05/feds-autopilot-was-active-during-deadly-march-tesla-crash/.

human drivers would stop and rubberneck. Tesla must have millions of examples of cars changing lanes suddenly or stopping short, but a perpendicular semi probably happens at most once a year, and even then, Tesla can't be there every time to collect data on it. Their data didn't include this outlier, and thus their model was incomplete in a way that had devastating consequences. Machine learning, in general, has an incredibly difficult time with exceptions and outliers. A well-designed AI system has a fallback option that doesn't rely on machine learning to deal with outlier scenarios.

Even for more common cases, data completeness can be difficult to achieve. For example, car crashes occur more frequently at night and during bad weather, so an autonomous self-driving system should certainly be trained to recognize dangerous scenarios in those contexts. But precisely because it's more dangerous to drive in those conditions, people drive in them less frequently, which means a lot less data exists to use for training.

Of course, the problem isn't restricted to self-driving cars. Credit card companies, for example, often have difficulty gathering enough examples of fraudulent transactions to train a model to detect them reliably. The vast majority of transactions aren't fraudulent, and those that are can have patterns that vary widely. For these companies, achieving completeness is a huge challenge.

In order to get closer to completeness in training data, Tesla and companies like it now focus on those edge cases directly, often generating synthetic data for outlier scenarios by creating them with simulators. This approach is imperfect—it means they have to predict anomalous situations before they happen—but it can help to fill holes in the data that could lead to fatal consequences.

When you create your initial specification document detailing the strategies and decisions that should be used when annotating your data and building your model, you'll also need to include all the anticipated edge cases the model is intended to support. If you don't intend to cover a known edge case, document that too. Without explicit documentation of these decisions, it will be extremely difficult to ensure that your data is complete down the line.

SECURITY

A popular online eyeglasses retailer needed a way to match its traditional brick-and-mortar competition, which allowed a customer to try on many pairs of glasses, look in the mirror, and check how they look in different lighting before actually making a purchase. One of the main challenges of the online company was to overcome customers' reluctance to buy something they would wear every day without trying it on.

To combat this reluctance, the company was developing a rich, augmented reality mobile app that would let a customer try on glasses virtually, using the camera on their phone. To accomplish this, they needed to annotate a huge dataset of people's faces, identifying different points on the face and how eyeglasses would sit on them.

As they embarked upon the project, security was a huge issue. A leak of the data they were annotating would damage their business by giving their competitors clues as to what they were working on. They were trying to create something innovative by solving a difficult problem. But if the data were stolen, their competitor could begin work on the same thing, and their competitive advantage—a comparatively short time to market—would evaporate.

A leak would also bring up privacy concerns. As we mentioned earlier, a leak of sensitive data can cause issues of trust even when the company is protected from legal liability. You may have explicitly acknowledged Facebook's right to redistribute images you upload as part of your membership agreement, but if your and your friends' faces started showing up on billboards without your consent, Facebook would have a significant PR problem on its hands. A good rule of thumb when it comes to data privacy is: just because you can doesn't mean you should.

It's important to document the regulations or industry standards you'll need to comply with, as well as any restrictions on your usage of the data. Knowing these up front will allow you to judge risks later that could take you out of compliance—for example, you might want to ignore a legally optional industry standard, but that may mean restricting your ability to enter a market. You'll need to outline these contours ahead of time in order to craft a plan to achieve your ultimate goals.

GOVERNANCE

Data, as we mentioned earlier, is the new IP. It's an incredibly important asset for your company, and its use has to be managed accordingly. Otherwise, inconsistencies or misuses of the data will cause problems down the line.

Companies that implement governance effectively set up internal policies that control how data is collected, transformed, and used, ensuring it is trustworthy and that the ways it can be used are clear.

The entire chain of custody of your data should be documented, from the contents of the dataset to the manner in which it was collected to the transformations that have been applied at each step along the way. Without this documentation, models that might be built relying on this data are unaware of the ways the data has been manipulated. The results of that model could end up being inconsistent or flat-out wrong.

In 2011, Jeremy Howard won a Kaggle® competition to build a model for the University of Melbourne that could predict the success of grant applications. To build his solution, he used a random forest algorithm to identify which fields in the data contributed most to a grant being approved.[53]

Unfortunately, Jeremy was unaware that the data had been transformed slightly from its original state; fields that had been left blank in the original grant applications had been labeled as having a null value instead of being ignored. As a result, he found that the biggest factor contributing to a grant's approval was the number of null fields. This technically won the contest in the way the rules were outlined, but because it bore no relation to an actual grant approval process, the solution wasn't of any use to the University of Melbourne. The data had been "cleaned," a helpful act, but because Jeremy didn't know it had been, he drew a conclusion and built a model that was useless.

Managing and documenting the chain of custody is also vital for security. It should be very clear at every stage

53 Kaggle, "Jeremy Howard on winning the Predict Grant Applications Competition", February 2011, https://medium.com/kaggle-blog/ jeremy-howard-on-winning-the-predict-grant-applications-competition-e70a252946c9.

who is able to read and who is able to modify the dataset. Besides preventing leaks, it can be vital for policy compliance.

In 2019, British Airways® was fined £183 million for a data breach that exposed personally identifiable information for around 500,000 of its customers.[54] The new (at the time) GDPR rules allowed a company to be fined a maximum of four percent of its worldwide revenue. Because British Airways' governance was insufficient to surface either their lax security or the liability to the company it introduced, they paid a huge price.

You'll need to tailor your governance program based on the size of your company, the level of AI maturity your company has, and the complexity of your data's journey. Governance can be huge and sophisticated, or small and simple.

No matter the size of your company, the success of any governance framework depends on visible buy-in from the executive team. This might mean the appointment of a chief data officer in a larger company; a smaller company might assign the role to the CTO or chief product officer.

---

54 Irwin, Luke, "British Airways to receive £20 million fine after ICO climbdown", *IT Governance Blog*, October 2020, https://www.itgovernance.co.uk/blog/british-airways-faces-sky-high-183-million-gdpr-fine#:~:text=British%20Airways%20to%20receive%20£20%20million%20fine%20after%20ICO%20climbdown&text=More%20than%20two%20years%20after,a%20£20%20million%20fine.

In either case, that person will need the public support of everyone on the company's executive team. It's important to promote a good governance mindset as a part of a company's culture since it'll be every employee's responsibility to implement it.

Large companies will need to establish a dedicated data governance team, who can keep track of and enforce data quality and documentation. Efficient governance spans the entire company and requires coordination among every team; at a huge company, it'll be too large a job for each department to assign to someone as a part-time responsibility.

Smaller companies, which probably can't afford the overhead of a dedicated team, can implement a lighter-weight process by setting up some basic principles. They can have a company-wide effort to develop the mindset to pay attention to data quality and security in the normal course of business.

Don't be afraid to start small; something is definitely better than nothing. Even in the absence of a holistic, broad investment and strategy from the top down, a company can develop pockets of strong governance through the efforts of individual contributors. If this is your situation, talk about it with your manager and find a way to make progress on the issue. Even something as small as writing down the data you're using to train a model will put the company in a better place.

DRIFT

In April 2016, Facebook introduced a new feature called Facebook Live. Users could just start recording and broadcasting themselves. Facebook didn't have a specific goal in mind for its use; they thought it would be a cool addition to the normal video upload features, and they'd see what people did with it. With that in mind, they deployed the same content moderation filters that applied to non-live video uploads.

Disturbingly, in 2019, a man used the feature to livestream himself massacring dozens of people in a mosque in Christchurch, New Zealand.[55] He was able to broadcast this horrible scene for 17 minutes before Facebook was notified of the situation and could disable it. The content moderation filters for Facebook videos didn't catch it because they hadn't anticipated this kind of horrific content being displayed. The data they'd used to train their content moderation filters and models in the past had drifted and no longer accurately reflected the inputs the system was being given. Something new had happened

---

55   Lapowsky, Issie, "Why Tech Didn't Stop the New Zealand Attack From Going Viral", *Wired*, March 2019, https://www.wired.com/story/new-zealand-shooting-video-social-media/.

in the world that was materially different from the way it had been visually organized before.

Before the 2016 US presidential election, the word "trump" had a particular meaning in the English language: to beat out competition and rank first in a contest. But as the 2016 election season progressed, its usage as the name of the Republican nominee for president and eventual electee became much more common. All the sentiment and intent and natural language processing models that categorized data from the news and social media had to be retrained in a hurry because the colloquial use of the word shifted so suddenly and dramatically.

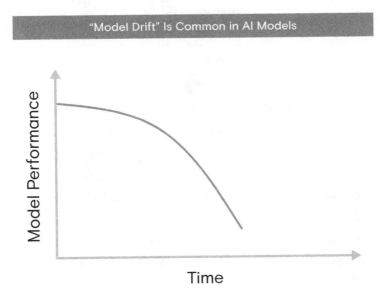

"Model Drift" Is Common in AI Models

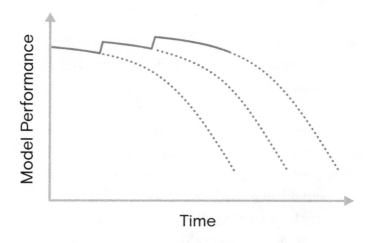

It's a good idea to refresh models at least monthly (if not more, depending on your use case; some models are updated as often as every day) to account for data drift. Drift can occur normally as a result of scale; as uses of the model expand, the set of possible inputs will naturally diverge from the original training data. Drift may also occur as a result of a major event, such as the Christchurch shooting or the 2016 US presidential election.

Even with good data governance, data can drift faster than the normal cadence of updates. More frequently, data governance is applied inconsistently. Many models are rolled into production without a responsible plan in place for updating and retraining periodically.

Change happens, and time passes. That's normal. Therefore, it's appropriate to put processes in place to account for iterating and learning. Just as a human learns over time to make better decisions informed by experience, your model should grow and improve as novel or changing information becomes available.

Every IT department monitors the performance of the infrastructure and software under its purview, but many companies neglect to monitor the performance of AI products after their launch. Because, as we've seen, the data and model can drift, it's vital to put in place a team and process to continue monitoring the model's performance.

Ownership of monitoring drift will live at more than one level, and it's a best practice to monitor for drift at all layers of the business. The data scientist may monitor some technical aspects of the model, and a business owner may monitor higher-level business performance. It's important to build a regular audit of model performance into your initial strategy.

By design, your decision-making criteria should learn to adapt to the introduction of new concepts. It's critical to start with the premise that things will change and work backward. In doing so, you'll build in flexibility and an ability to adapt to that change.

No matter what, these problems can be hard to solve. YouTube had an enormous budget and the best technology, yet still planned for change by including humans in the ongoing feedback loop. It will take iteration and persistence, but as long as you do your best to develop a responsible, adaptable data strategy at the outset, you'll be well-positioned to handle the change that will inevitably come your way.

CHAPTER 10

BUILD OR BUY?

"Artificial Intelligence, deep learning, machine learning — whatever you're doing if you don't understand it — learn it. Because otherwise you're going to be a dinosaur within three years."

—MARK CUBAN

A big question when introducing AI into your organization is whether you're going to build the model in-house or purchase components from a third-party vendor and integrate them into your business. To build an AI system, the following steps need to be provided by a team within your organization:

- Acquire training data
- Label training data
- Train model
- Validate model offline

- Deploy the model to production
- A/B testing model performance (optional)
- Monitor the model in production
- Refresh the model regularly (optional)

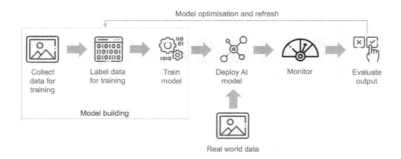

There are also several technical components necessary for a successful AI system that your team will need to build. These technical components are as follows:

- Data Collection and Annotation Platform: this is the platform that is used to collect and label training data.
- Training Data Management Platform: this is the platform that is used to keep and manage all the training data. The training data can be acquired from a third-party vendor (e.g., image data collected by third-party vendors) or from internal data (e.g., transaction data from a data warehouse). This is either part of the company's internal data lake/data warehouse or closely integrated with the data lake/data warehouse.
- Machine Learning Training Platform: this is the plat-

form used to train and debug machine learning models. It can have tools or frameworks like TensorFlow or Pytorch and also be connected to a training data management platform to feed data into those tools, debug the model, and validate model performance offline.

- Machine Learning Inference Platform: this is the platform where machine learning models are deployed and used to make predictions. It can be a production environment, where other applications can interact with it through real-time API calls, or an environment where operation people can run non-real-time batch jobs.
- Feature Store: this is the place where machine learning models get real-time feature data and use them as inputs to conduct model prediction.
- MLOps System: the system used by dev-ops teams to deploy the model, refresh the model, and monitor the model's performance.

It may be more appropriate for your organization to purchase and integrate AI components. If so, it's important not to underestimate all the components you'll need to be successful with machine learning. You also can't just buy a complete solution off the shelf. There's no one-stop-shop that can provide you with the entire system you need. Your company will have to invest in some components to support an AI solution, but the work you put in will consist of strategizing carefully on what to buy.

The first step in this strategy should be to consider the core value that you provide to your customers. What is it they value or prize when they transact with you instead of your competitors? Why don't they do what you do themselves?

The core values of your organization should flow through into every downstream project. These values will help guide you as you make decisions about what is or isn't core in a technical evaluation. If something gives you a competitive advantage, you may want to build it in-house. If, on the other hand, your focus is to serve your customers in the immediate term, it may make more sense to buy it. Even if your competitors buy the same product, you can mitigate that risk by maintaining the quality and value of your data.

Take the fashion retailer with the sweater blazer from earlier. When they started implementing AI solutions to provide higher value to their customers, it would have been a bad use of their time and money to create technical infrastructure from scratch. It has nothing to do with their core competency—fashion. It also wouldn't have provided them with an advantage over their competitors, nor enhanced their brand. They were better off buying off-the-shelf solutions for most or all of the infrastructure.

A major facet of Apple's brand is security. One of the reasons some people buy an iPhone over an Android phone is Apple's reputation for taking security and privacy very seriously. The Photos app on an iPhone uses facial recognition to identify the people in photos and organize them accordingly. When that feature makes a mistake and misidentifies a woman as her sister or mom, it's an amusing inconvenience with no real harm done. It's easy to understand how the machine learning algorithm could get confused between sisters in photos. However, when Apple introduced Face ID as a method of unlocking your phone, many users were disappointed to discover that their phones recognized their siblings' faces to unlock. Even though the technology used is similar to the Photos app, users were frustrated and upset. It was a major hit to a core part of Apple's brand—security.[56]

It's not public information whether Apple built or bought the technology backing these features, but while they might have made the decision to buy the facial recognition model that powers the photos feature, it would have been in their best interest to take greater control of the model that powers Face ID. The feature is more sensitive, and its function speaks directly to Apple's brand.

There are many reasons that could drive a company to buy a component off the shelf, even if it does affect their

56 Dickey, Megan Rose. "PSA: Don't Train Face ID on Your Sibling's Face Accidentally." *TechCrunch*, TechCrunch, 5 Nov. 2017, techcrunch.com/2017/11/05/psa-dont-train-face-id-on-your-siblings-face-accidentally/.

core business. Often, companies will be tempted to take a shortcut to reduce their time to market if they see or anticipate competitors about to do the same.

In some other cases, it may be prohibitively expensive to build a team to create infrastructure from scratch. When Yahoo!® was making a similar decision, they were concerned that they wouldn't be able to hire enough talent for a machine learning team to work on their core search functionality. Facing pressure to stay competitive in the short term, they chose to stop investing in search as a core business.[57] Of course, history has shown that Yahoo! lost that one to Google.

When you start making the decision to build or buy, you'll need to first understand your problem, as well as the strategic value of solving it. Both building and buying require money and investment, so you'll also need to understand the budget you have in the context of the value your solution will provide to the company.

Consider the role time and urgency in your decision. Shortening the time to market may be a priority. The opportunity costs of not solving the problem may be significant. Both options, building and buying, have time-

---

57   Lam, Bourree, "Taking Stock of Yahoo in Its Final Days as a Public Company", *The Atlantic*, April 2017, https://www.theatlantic.com/business/archive/2017/04/yahoo-verizon-public/523599/.

lines associated with them—you might be able to buy and implement a component in half the time it would take you to build it yourself.

You'll also have to examine the quality of a particular solution. If you buy an off-the-shelf component, of course you'd evaluate its quality. But even if other considerations have you tending toward building a component in-house, if you don't have the technical sophistication, resources, or expertise to build it with sufficient quality, that option might be off the table.

You might think that buying a third-party product and integrating it deeply into your business has the potential to introduce security risks. But unless you have significant security expertise internally, you could just as easily introduce those risks by building insecure functionality.

Finally, consider whether dedicating resources to something, even a core competency of your organization, will distract from other key investments or strategies. Apple could dedicate huge amounts of resources to building the best facial recognition security system in the world, but would that distract too much from the business of building its core products?

All of these considerations will play into the ultimate decision. But don't worry; building or buying one part of the

AI supply chain doesn't mean the rest of the pieces need to follow suit. You can build a part of your AI solution while buying other components. There are many pieces of major infrastructure you'll need to set up to enable your eventual success, but they can integrate in any number of ways that will support your competing priorities.

The first piece of infrastructure, of course, is your data, along with a data pipeline and a data warehouse. As we've discussed in previous chapters, you'll need to have a lot of data to feed your model, as well as a way to clean it, move it, organize it, and store it. Unless you have extremely specific needs, there are many open source and commercial products that can handle the mechanics of moving data from here to there.

You'll also need infrastructure that enables you to annotate all your data, which will integrate with your data pipeline. In some cases, the annotations you provide will be the key differentiator that allows your model to provide business value, which might convince you to build this infrastructure yourself to protect your IP. But many commercial companies, such as Appen, already have security solutions in place to protect your data, as well as the processes and knowledge to help you annotate your data most effectively.

Next, you'll need a platform to orchestrate training, testing, and hosting your models. All of the major cloud platforms—Amazon, Google, Microsoft—provide machine learning platforms that can automatically train, test, tune, and deploy models. There are also full life cycle open source solutions, like Kubeflow®, as well as point solutions that can be integrated together or with components you build yourself. And, of course, commercial vendors like Databricks can build more sophisticated custom solutions.

You'll have to think deeply about whether to build or buy each of these pieces of infrastructure, but if you consider your core values up front and understand the value of the problem you're solving, you'll be able to find the right solution. Other things being equal, you should try to build components that are key to your company's core business and buy the rest.

CONCLUSION

"It is not your responsibility to finish the work of perfecting the world, but you are not free to desist from it either."

—RABBI TARFON, PIRKE AVOT 2:21

To take AI from concept to real-world use, you need to define a sound AI strategy, build the right organization, pick the right pilot problem, and scale sensibly to production. Now that you've read this book, you have everything you need to make that happen.

If you put the techniques and advice we've described in this book into practice, your pilot project will be much more likely to make it into production, solve a real business problem, and show the rest of your organization just what AI can do. At the same time, you'll have taken huge steps toward instituting the organization and infrastructure you need to enable long-term AI success.

Sophisticated, thoughtful curation of data is critical to the success of your AI integration. You have to ensure you are using the right data that has been thoughtfully curated and organized to meet your specific business needs. The data must be responsibly sourced and applied. You must also thoroughly consider the data so that unwanted bias does not seep into your system.

You now understand how essential it will be to secure continued access to high-quality training data. So many people believe the hardest part of AI is building the model, only to learn how wrong they are when they deploy to production and watch their model's performance degrade because they didn't know they had to retrain continuously as the world changed around the model. You, however, know how to avoid similar pitfalls.

Hopefully, you've gained the confidence to get involved directly in the building of your solution, even if you don't have a technical background. As a businessperson, your participation is absolutely critical to your organization's success. AI projects often fail, but if you implement these best practices, you'll be able to test and deploy a system that works for your business, your users, and society at large.

We also hope you've developed an understanding of the high degree of ethical consideration that should accompany your efforts. Machine learning is an extremely powerful technology and extremely easy to use irresponsibly. The decision to harness this technology for your business or organization is a step into the future, but you must also make a commitment to do the requisite work necessary to use it ethically and sensibly. Before you play with fire, you have to learn how to handle it so it doesn't cause more harm than good.

No matter how you deploy machine learning, you are deploying bias at scale. By definition, you are encoding bias and decision-making into a very big, fancy engine that is going to make decisions on behalf of a human. When you participate in the creation of this engine, you have a basic moral obligation to do so responsibly. Now that you've read this book, you have the foundation to start off on your path in the right direction.

This can all sound intimidating and overwhelming, but there's no reason to be afraid of AI. It's not magic, and it's not even rocket science. With hard work and the right team working together collaboratively, you can do this, and you can do it well. Now, roll up your sleeves and get started!

Take the AI readiness quiz: appen.com/ai-readiness-score

GLOSSARY

A/B testing

A controlled, real-life experiment designed to compare two variants of a system or a model, A and B.

algorithm

A set of rules a machine (and especially a computer) follows to achieve a particular goal.

annotation

A note of explanation, label, or comment added to a piece of data like audio, text, or image.

artificial intelligence

The theory and development of computer systems able to

perform tasks that normally require human intelligence, such as visual perception, speech recognition, decision-making, and translation between languages.

artificial neural network

An architecture composed of successive layers of simple connected units called artificial neurons interweaved with nonlinear activation functions, which is vaguely reminiscent of the neurons in an animal brain.

bounding box

The smallest (rectangular) box fully containing a set of points or an object. Used to train computer vision systems to detect objects.

chatbot

A computer program or an AI designed to interact with human users through conversation.

classification

The systematic arrangement in groups or categories according to established criteria.

clustering

Grouping a set of objects so that objects within the same group (called a cluster) are more "similar" to each other than they are to those in other groups.

computer vision

The field of machine learning that studies how to gain high-level understanding from images or videos.

confidence threshold (interval)

A type of interval estimate that is likely to contain the true value of an unknown population parameter. The interval is associated with a confidence level that quantifies the level of confidence of this parameter being in the interval.

contributor

A human worker who provides annotations on a data platform.

data

A piece of information.

Unstructured data: raw, unprocessed data. Textual data, images, or audio is a perfect example of unstructured data because it is not formatted or annotated into specific organizational framework or classifications.

Structured data: data processed in a way that it becomes ingestible by a machine learning algorithm and, if in the case of supervised machine learning, labeled data.

Data augmentation: the process of adding new information derived from both internal and external sources to a dataset, typically through annotation.

decision tree

A category of supervised machine learning algorithms where the data is iteratively split in respect to a given parameter or criteria.

deep learning

A broader family of machine learning methods based on learning data representations, as opposed to task-specific algorithms. Deep learning can be supervised, semi-supervised, or unsupervised.

feature

A variable that is used as an input to a model.

false negative

A test result that incorrectly indicates that a particular condition or attribute is absent.

false positive

A test result which incorrectly indicates that a particular condition or attribute is present.

garbage in, garbage out

A principle stating that whenever the input data is flawed, it will lead to misleading results and produces nonsensical output, AKA "garbage".

General Data Protection Regulation (GDPR)

A regulation in EU law on data protection and privacy for all individuals within the European Union aiming to give control to citizens and residents over their personal data.

inference

The process of making predictions by applying a trained model to new, unlabeled instances.

machine learning

The subfield of artificial intelligence that often uses statistical techniques to give computers the ability to "learn", i.e., progressively improve performance on a specific task, with data, without being explicitly programmed.

model

An abstracted representation of what a machine learning system has learned from the training data during the training process.

natural language processing

The area of artificial intelligence that studies the interactions between computers and human languages, in particular how to process and analyze large amounts of natural language data.

neural network

See artificial neural network.

optical character recognition (OCR)

The conversion of images of printed, handwritten, or typed text into a machine-friendly textual format. A subset of computer vision.

optimization

The selection of the best element (with regard to some criterion) from some set of available alternatives.

personally identifiable information

Any piece of information that can be used on its own or in combination with some other information in order to identify a particular individual.

prediction

The inferred output of a trained model provided with an input instance.

regression

A set of statistical processes for estimating the relationships among variables.

reinforcement learning

The subfield of machine learning inspired by human behavior that studies how an agent ought to take action in a given environment to maximize some notion of cumulative reward.

speech recognition

A subfield of machine learning and computational linguistics interested in methods that enables the recognition and translation of spoken language into text by computers. Everyday examples of speech recognition power Apple Siri, Amazon Alexa or Google Home.

supervised learning

The machine learning task of learning a function mapping an input to an output based on example input-output pairs.

TensorFlow®

An open-source library, popular among the machine learning community, for data flow programming across a range of tasks. It is a symbolic math library and is also used for machine learning applications such as neural networks.

testing

In the context of supervised machine learning, the process of assessing the final performance of a model using hold-out data.

Testing data: The subset of available data that a data scientist selected for the testing phase of the development of a model.

training data

In the context of supervised machine learning, the construction of algorithms that can learn from and make predictions from data.

Training data: The subset of available data that a data scientist selected for the training phase of the development of a model.

unsupervised learning

The area of machine learning that consists of inferring a function that describes the structure of unlabeled data.

ACKNOWLEDGMENTS

One of the wonderful things about the machine learning space is the willingness and culture of so many to share expertise, lessons learned, and new ideas with others. This book would not have been possible without the guidance of so many who have encouraged us in our respective careers in small and large ways—teaching us, challenging our assumptions, and guiding our paths. Thank you to Kareem Yusuf, Marty Cagan, Tara Lemmey, Elliot Turner, Manish Goyal, John R. Smith, Matthew Hill, Beth Smith, John Schumacher, Rama Akkiraju, Benjamin Kearns, Hugh Williams, Andy Edmonds, Mike Mathieson, Zoher Karu, Dan Fain, David Goldberg, and Bala Meduri.

We would like to acknowledge the many people who helped contribute to making this book a reality: Jon Kondo, Sid Mistry, Titus Capilnean, Stevi Rex, Meghan McCracken, Christina Golden, and the entire team at Scribe Publishng for their writing, editing, and guidance on how to turn anecdotes and stories into an actual book, as well as Appen for the opportunity to put this all together. Thanks to Lukas Biewald, Stacey Ronaghan, Ramkumar Ravichandran, Hernan Alvarez, Kris Skrinak, Brooke Wenig, B. Cavello, Patrick McDermott, Yochay Ettun, Aaron Zukoff, Kareena Manji, Matthew Mirick, Vaishali Rana, and Jean-Luis Caamano for sharing their wisdom and stories with us for publication.

To our partners and families who love us unconditionally, we would be nowhere without you. We certainly wouldn't have been able to find the time to write a book without your unwavering support—thank you for all that you do.

ABOUT THE AUTHORS

ALYSSA SIMPSON ROCHWERGER is a customer-driven product leader dedicated to building products that solve hard problems for real people. She delights in bringing products to market that make a positive impact for customers. Her experience in scaling products from concept to large-scale ROI has been proven at both startups and large enterprises alike.

She has held numerous product leadership roles for machine learning organizations. She served as VP of product for Figure Eight (acquired by Appen), VP of AI and data at Appen, and director of product at IBM Watson. She recently left the space to pursue her dream of using technology to improve healthcare. Currently, she serves as director of product at Blue Shield of California, where she is happily surrounded by lots of data, many hard problems, and nothing but opportunities to make a positive impact.

he is thrilled to pursue the mission of providing access to high-quality, affordable healthcare that is worthy of our families and friends.

Alyssa was born and raised in San Francisco, California, and holds a BA in American studies from Trinity College. When she is not geeking out on data and technology, she can be found hiking, cooking, and dining at "off the beaten path" restaurants with her family.

WILSON PANG joined Appen in November 2018 as CTO and is responsible for the company's products and technology. Wilson has over nineteen years' experience in software engineering and data science. Prior to joining Appen, Wilson was chief data officer of Ctrip in China, the second-largest online travel agency company in the world, where he led data engineers, analysts, data product managers, and scientists to improve user experience and increase operational efficiency that grew the business. Before that, he was senior director of engineering at eBay in California and provided leadership in various domains, including data service and solutions, search science, marketing technology, and billing systems. He worked as an architect at IBM prior to eBay, building technology solutions for various clients.

Wilson obtained his master's and bachelor's degrees in electrical engineering from Zhejiang University in China.

CPSIA information can be obtained
at www.ICGtesting.com
Printed in the USA
LVHW091911030421
683375LV00001B/2